Onionheads

A Tragi-Comedy by

JESSE MILLER

*Winner of the 1999
Kennedy Center American College Theatre Festival
National Student Playwriting Award*

SAMUEL FRENCH, INC.

45 WEST 25TH STREET   NEW YORK 10010

7623 SUNSET BOULEVARD   HOLLYWOOD 90046

LONDON   *TORONTO*

ISBN 0 573 62723 1   Printed in U.S.A.   #17720

IMPORTANT BILLING AND CREDIT REQUIREMENTS

All producers of ONIONHEADS *must* give credit to the Author of the Play in all programs distributed in connection with performances of the Play and in all instances in which the title of the Play appears for purposes of advertising, publicizing or otherwise exploiting the Play and/or a production. The name of the Author *must* also appear on a separate line, on which no other name appears, immediately following the title, and *must* appear in size of type not less than fifty percent the size of the title type.

MUSIC PERMISSION INFORMATION

"So long, it's been good to know yuh" (Woody Guthrie @ The Richmond Organization, New York) Permission for the use must be secured from Folkways Music Publishers, Inc., c/o The Richmond Organization, 11 West 19th Street, New York, NY 10011-4298

"Do Re Mi" (Woody Guthrie @ The Richmond Organization, New York) Permission for the use must be secured from Ludlow Music, Inc., c/o The Richmond Organization, 11 West 19th Street, New York, NY 10011-4298

"Leavin' Blues" (aka "Grasshoppers in My Pillow") (Huddie Ledbetter/Leadbelly @ The Richmond Organization, New York) Permission for the use must be secured from Folkways Music Publishers, Inc., c/o The Richmond Organization, 11 West 19th Street, New York, NY 10011-4298

"Hard Times" (Stephen Collins Foster), "Clementine" and "Hush Little Baby" (Public Domain)

ONIONHEADS
is the winner of the
1999 KC/ACTF National Student Playwriting Award

ONIONHEADS
was first presented at
California Institute of the Arts
for
The New Plays Festival
and then at the
Kennedy Center
for the
American College Theatre Festival XXXI

Scenic Design by Nick May and Jesse Miller
Lighting Design by Clay Alexander
Sound Design by Mike Fricassi
Costumes designed by Pascaline Bellegarde
Stage Manager   Stacy Deckard
Assistant Stage Manager   Pam Buzick

Directed by
Pascaline Bellegarde and Jesse Miller

CAST
(in order of appearance)

Dusty	Jesse Miller
Jeb Tidwell	Bengt Anderson
Aloysius Tidwell	Oen Armstrong
Penny Bumpinmeyer	Amanda Freund
Clementine Bumpinmeyer	Amber Skalski

CHARACTERS

DUSTY: 25 or older, mysterious banjo player, the devil himself

JEB TIDWELL: 20, cynical, caretaker, skirt chaser, onion picker

ALOYSIUS TIDWELL: 18, childlike, idealistic, mama's boy, onion picker

PENNY BUMPINMEYER: 20, strong, beautiful, sassy, onion picker

CLEMENTINE BUMPINMEYER: 17, quirky, awkward, emotional, onion picker

ACT I

Time: July, 1935
Place: Tidwell Farm / Hooker, Oklahoma

ACT II

Scene 1

Time: October, 1935
Place: Route 66 (Brothers)
Imperial Valley Migrant Camp, California (Sisters)

Scene 2

Time: November, 1935
Place: Imperial Valley Migrant Camp, California

For Betty and Erma

ACT I

(July, 1935. The Tidwell Farm, Hooker, Oklahoma.
In a dim dusty orange light, a saggin' farmhouse porch holds two
tired ol' chairs, a-settin' to the tune of the screen door slammin'
in the win'. A chime mobile made from bent spoons is singin'. A
rusty scythe an' pitchfork lay against the house as if they was
leanin' on their mother for comfort. The Hooker farm sobs with
depression an' sufferin'. An eerie breeze whispers through the
faded flowered dress, a huge dingy brassiere, an' ol' stockin's,
hangin' on the clothesline. There is a feelin' that somepin evil is
suffocatin' the strugglin' homestead. STUMP, a stuffed dead
yella Labrador, sets stiffly by a naked tree; he never ever moves,
ever. The mutt holds a last expression of hopelessness, causin'
one to wonder what the poor fella saw to bring his face such sad-
ness.
A spotlight, like a shaft of sunlight, fin's DUSTY as he sets on a tree
stump with a raggedy banjo. He devilishly plunks the Woody
Guthrie folk tune, "So long, it's been good to know yuh."*
He looks up slowly, as if he is a calculated killer, an' begins ironic'lly
singin' a folk song. His lips hold a smug expression an' his eyes
have the arrogance of conquest.)

DUSTY.
"Wellll, I've sung this song, but I'll sing it again,
Of the people I've met an' the places I've been,
In the month of April, the county called Gray,
Here's what all of the people there say,

———

*See page three for information on obtaining permission to use this song.

'So long, it's been good to know yuh,
So long, it's been good to know yuh,
So long, it's been good to know yuh,
This dusty ol' dust is a-gettin' my home,
I've got to be driftin' along.'

The telephone rang an' it jumped off the wall,
That was the preacher, a-makin' his call,
He said, 'Kind friend, this may be the end,
You've got your last chance of salvation of sin.'

So long, it's been good to know yuh,
So long, it's been good to know yuh,
So long, it's been good to know yuh,
This dusty ol' dust is a-gettin' my home,
An' I've got to be driftin' along...

The churches was jammed and the churches was packed,
And that dusty old dust storm blowed so black,
The preacher could not read a word of his text,
So he folded his specs and he took up collections, said,

So long, it's been good to know yuh,
So long, it's been good to know yuh,
So long, it's been good to know yuh,
This dusty ol' dust is a-gettin' my home,
And I've got to be driftin' along."

(The win' roars. The spoon chimes clang their moody groan. DUSTY
stops playin' an' goes to the edge of the dyin' fiel'. He picks a
dried, shriveled onion, sniffs it for potency, then drops it an'
laughs inta the mouth of the approachin' dust storm...The farm
goes black. DUSTY disappears. The win' dies an' the sun beats
down.
JEB TIDWELL, 20, comes outta the house onto the porch, coughin'
through a faded red kerchief, which he wears over his mouth. He
squints to see the doomed onion crops that surroun' the Tidwell

*farm. Dressed in a true "Depression ensemble," an' plen'y of
arrogance to fill his wiry frame, JEB pulls his kerchief down an'
picks a dried-up weed to chew. Silence. He stan's at the edge of
the fiel' an' sighs at the blackness he sees before him.*
ALOYSIUS TIDWELL, 18, JEB'S *brother, sportin' overalls an' a tattered hat, backs onto the porch like he's jus' been tickled. He
hollers upstairs to* MAMA, *who ain't never seen.)*

ALOYSIUS. *(To MAMA.)* …Mama, I cain't eat me no more onion cakes er I'll burst like a tick in a battlefiel'!… My belly needs
some understandin'…. Aw, don't cry Mama…. Jus' gimme time to git
steady an' you can puff me up again come lunchtime…. Is 'at a smile
makin' itself at home on yer ruby doll lips? It is! Now who loves you
more 'an anythin' on God's green earth?… 'At's right!… An' who's
gonna grab a piece a the moon down so's you can be all lit like an angel ferever an' ever an' ever…? 'At's right again! Now you go rest yer
purty little head in 'at mornin' nap you speak so highly of. Jeb an' me,
we got pickin' ta do. *(To JEB.)* Ain't we brother?! *(To MAMA.)*
Kisses, Mama. An' push them wet towels in the grin of them windas
so's you can dream real good like. K? K. *(Sees STUMP, the dog.)*
Stump's on the lookout fer our friend, Mister Win'. GOOD BOY!
*(Beat. ALOYSIUS searches for his own weed, but on'y fin's a large
twig. He chews on it, imitatin' his brother. The two boys stan' together at the edge of the fiel', like opposite sides of the same coin.
The twig brushes JEB'S face. Annoyed, JEB, breaks it in half an'
places it back in his brother's mouth. Beat. ALOYSIUS smiles at the
crop.)* Jeb?

JEB. Yep.
ALOYSIUS. Mornin'.
JEB. Yep.
ALOYSIUS. Purty one.
JEB. Yep.
ALOYSIUS. *(Beat.)* Yep.
JEB. Yep. *(Beat.)* Dust on the porch again, an' they says it's on'y
gonna git worse.
ALOYSIUS. Who's sayin' 'at?

JEB. Papa. Papa said it.

(JEB gives a matter-of-fact look to his brother, then goes to set in his porch chair.)

ALOYSIUS. Well, they's yer problem right'chere. Papa's playin' a joke on you, jus' fer ducks, silly! 'Member when Papa said he'd rather have pigs than children, 'cause when they's all growed-up, you can eat all the slop you put in 'em? Now Papa didn' mean 'at. An' 'member when Papa went out in the rain an' offered you an' me up to God fer jus' a measly quart a tapioca? Papa didn' mean 'at, neither, sure as I's a-settin' here. *(Realizin' he ain't a-settin' at all, ALOYSIUS sets.)* You got yerself a bad case a lis'nin', 'at's all. See, me, I jus' take it all in me, an' then shuck it like a ripe piece a corn. You git the icky part off, then you eat the good part. See Jeb, you gotta hear 'tween the lines. I could learn you how in no time.

JEB. Ain't jus' Papa. It's the lan'. She's speakin' to us, chokin' us so's we cain't rob her no more.

ALOYSIUS. *(Proudly lookin' at crop.)* It's true. Lan' *can* talk up a storm. Ain't got no mouth er nothin'.

JEB. How about Buck Cloverdale?

ALOYSIUS. Now, he got a mouth!

JEB. As we set here dreamin'— Buck an' his fam'ly is in 'at broken down ol' Ford headin' to pick a future in Califor-nee. Imperial Valley, he said, along with the Andersons, the Knightens an' the Hotchkisses.

ALOYSIUS. The Blackflowers is stayin' put.

JEB. They's cotton farmers. They ain't got sense. Why, they pride themselves on standin' in the fiel', stuffin' their crop in their ears, blockin' out the rest of us who're speakin' the truth. I hollered to 'em once er twice. They jus' waved back all ignorant like, smilin'. Didn' hear a word I said. Savages.

ALOYSIUS. They's farmers, jus' the same.

JEB. Cain't count them. 'At cotton makes 'em insane. "Insane of the head they call it."

ALOYSIUS. So.

JEB. So, dust is comin', Aloysius. More black'n you ever seen, trappin' us 'til we cain't breathe no more. You can preten' all you want, be cotton crazy. But dust is comin'.

ALOYSIUS. Papa'll be back with supplies soon, an' we'll git through it, like we git through ever'thin' else. Mama tol' me 'at God is jus' testin' us, throwin' a little cinnamon on our pie. Mama tol' me. Mama's not leavin'. An' I'm not leavin' Mama. 'Sides, we got pickin' ta do.

(ALOYSIUS heads into the fiel'. JEB yells to stop him.)

JEB. Pickin' what? Those few stubborn onions 'at jus' cain't give up, like the fools down at the church prayin' fer the win' to stop? Cain't fight the devil, when he is the dust, an' the storm, an' the win'. An' I hates to say it, but the good Lord is chokin' on the evil, same as them onions … not a sin between 'em.

ALOYSIUS. Tidwell onions is the toughest in the whole wide world! *(Hollerin' to them onions.)* AN' AS LONG AS THEY'S WILLIN' TO GROW FER THIS FARM, I'M WILLIN' TO PICK 'EM! Loyal crop, 'at's what 'at is.

JEB. Loyal? Ha! Ain't nothin' loyal in this tired ol' town 'cept the sun 'at keeps risin' to torture me with the sight of a dyin' fiel' of strangled heads!

ALOYSIUS. *(Runnin' to talk to MAMA.)* Nothin' Mama!… Jeb was jus' tellin' me one a his sad stories…. Yep, the "strangled heads" one…. I knows, he loves tellin' 'at one…. Okey Dokey. Ni-night. *(To JEB.)* Mama says, "QUIT IT!" (*Beat. ALOYSIUS sets on the porch an' puts his worn-out shoes on. Seein' JEB deep in thought, he becomes curious.*) What'cha thinkin'?

JEB. Nothin'.

ALOYSIUS. Me too! How do you figger a thing like that there happens?

JEB. Jus' luck, I s'pose.

ALOYSIUS. Oh, it's more'n luck. *(Drawin' in the dust.)* Now, the way I sees it, you got my brain an' yer brain, comin' aroun' the bend with *nothin',* at exactly the same time! 'At's jus' "kin"…'at's what 'at is!

JEB. Yer drawin' in the dust, Aloysius.

(ALOYSIUS gits a look of horror an' blows his drawin' away.)

ALOYSIUS. Jus' dirt from my boots!

JEB. Yer drawin' in what's left a McKinney's farm at the edge a town. There she is, a-settin' on our front porch, spread out like Penny Bumpinmeyer on a Saturd'y night, laughin' at us, like she owns the place. An' we ain't got the looks er the money to pay her. 'At dust is heartless.

ALOYSIUS. Quit it Jeb! Quit teasin' about stuff like 'at! *(Whisperin'.)* I'm a-gonna tell Mama.

JEB. *(Playin' like he's spooked.)* Ooohhh.

ALOYSIUS. *(Imitatin' JEB.)* Oooohh.

JEB. *(Lookin' into fiel' with a serious expression.)* Oooooh. *(ALOYSIUS gits scairt with this one.)* What's 'at? Here she comes! Here comes the evil Dust Queen! She's a-gonna gitcha'!

(JEB chases ALOYSIUS aroun' the porch, spookin' him.)

ALOYSIUS. You don' wanna make me sore!

JEB. She's a-gonna huff an' puff an' blow yer house in, clean outta Hooker, by yer chinny chin chin! Ooooh, thar she blows! The state a Oklahoma is no more— Wooooosshh! Dust is comin' fer you, Aloysius, so's you can draw the whole goddamn bible in it!

(ALOYSIUS puts his fists up, then melts like a soybean in the sun when he hears MAMA.)

ALOYSIUS. Now you done it, Jeb! Mama heared you. *(ALOYSIUS rushes to door an' hollers to MAMA.)* No, Mama … Jeb's jus' playin' 'at game a his, 'at funny "Ghost chasin' Aloysius aroun' the porch 'til he's good an' scairt an' stuff," game, on accounta they ain't enough dust to draw nothin' in…. Not even the purty likes a you, Mama … an' 'at's a cryin' shame. *(Beat. ALOYSIUS whispers to JEB, angrily.)* Made me lie to Mama! Now, I's a-goin' to hell fer sure!

JEB. We's already livin' in it.

(ALOYSIUS walks to the clothesline, sees MAMA'S brassiere an' stockin's, an' quickly takes 'em down. He looks aroun' protectively an' strokes the undergarments as if MAMA herself was in them.)

ALOYSIUS. *(Happily.)* Warshed Mama's underthin's. I better bring 'em in, 'fore somebody sees 'em an' gits all riled-up.

(ALOYSIUS runs an' takes 'em inside.)

JEB. Aloysius! You shouldn' be handlin' Mama's ... *ladies'* skivvies, unless they ain't kin. Then it's ree-spectable ... an' downright admired, dependin' on the owner—
ALOYSIUS. *(Returnin' with a smile.)* Shoulda seen how happy Mama was to git *them* back.
JEB. Little brother! You need to ... to ... to git yerself a hobby er somepin.
ALOYSIUS. *(Beat.)* Awww ... I know why yer so awnry this mornin'.... Hey, is 'at a pimple, er a girl under yer skin? *(ALOYSIUS tickles JEB to the groun'. JEB giggles uncontrollably like a little boy.)* You dog! You must be gittin' yer share of a good woman!

(JEB rises an' tries to reclaim his cool demeanor. He gloats like a right proud rooster.)

JEB. Tell it like it is.
ALOYSIUS. Golly! It's Penny, ain't it?! Penny Bumpinmeyer! See how I knew 'at? 'At's "kin." 'At's what 'at is. "Kin-tuition!"
JEB. *(Coverin'.)* Aw, she ain't nothin' to me.
ALOYSIUS. Uh huh.

(ALOYSIUS smiles. They both set in the dirt, outta breath.)

JEB. She mise well be warshed from the face of the earth fer all I care.

ALOYSIUS. Uh huh. (*Beat.*) She still smoochin' on 'at Carl Crowbody? (*Admiringly.*) 'At fella's got the longest eyelashes I ever did see—like ... like butterfly wings. Butterfly wings—

(ALOYSIUS demonstrates on his eyes. JEB shoots him a look. ALOYSIUS recovers by drawin' in the dirt. JEB nonchalantly feels his own eyelashes fer length, but sighs at his short lashes. ALOYSIUS sighs to sympathize with JEB. Beat.)

JEB. I cain't even go to the diner no more ... people pointin' an' starin' at me like I's some kinda chump. 'An jus' to spite me, Penny dolls herself up, pinches color in 'er cheeks an' rats 'er hair up like a big ol' beacon, an' then wastes it on my best frien'! He don't 'preciate her like I do. The sacrifices I have made fer 'at woman! (*Confessin'.*) Aloysius, I use' ta save the fat Mama'd give Stump from a bad batch of bacon er somepin, wrap it up in my best kerchief, walk Penny on over to Badman's Pond like a cow on a rope, an' surprise 'er with it! Her papa wouldn' let 'er eat fat. Says 'er bone structure wouldn' take well to it, so she was always cravin' it real bad....So bad 'at she'd start to sal-ee-vate at the thought of it, like Stump does when you say "Bone bone!"

ALOYSIUS. (*Givin' STUMP a grandiose order.*) HEAL!

JEB. Penny use' ta beg me, — beg me jus' to use the word "fat" in a sentence.

ALOYSIUS. Golly ... like "Gee, Penny, yer gittin' real fat!" er somepin?

JEB. Yep. An' if that weren't enough, I carved our names in the ol' oak at Finney's Fork, an' let her rub the tension from my shoulders fer ... a couple a-three hours er so. Takes a lot a strength to carve "Bumpinmeyer" in a tree. T'ain't no lie.

ALOYSIUS. (*Proudly.*) Mama carved my name in the water pump— Carved "Mama loves Aloysius," on it, she did, in cursive, with Papa's pick ax. Woman can han'le a blade! She was a-whackin' away at it, an' she turned ta me an' said, "Aloysius, are you watchin' me a-whack away at this?" An' I says, "Yes, Mama!" 'cause I was ... an' she said, "Now ever'time you pump fer water, you know yer mama loves you." An' I do.

JEB. You was two, Aloysius.

ALOYSIUS. Uh huh.

JEB. Months.

ALOYSIUS. Uh huh.

JEB. T'ain' no way you could— *(ALOYSIUS smiles. It's no use. JEB gives in.)* Now 'at ol' pump's growed over'th moss an' ivy.

ALOYSIUS. Still gives you water jus' the same.

JEB. Well … I says it's time you was carvin' with yer manhood on the side a-somepin.

(JEB punches ALOYSIUS in the arm, an' laughs. ALOYSIUS looks at him with a blank expression. JEB drops his smile, gives up an' walks toward the fiel' an' sighs. Long beat. JEB flexes to check that he is still somepin to behold. ALOYSIUS stares inta the fiel' an' stiffens with fear, as suddenly, it hits him … the deep feelin's of the dyin' onions. ALOYSIUS whispers to JEB through his teeth.)

ALOYSIUS. Jeb?

JEB. Yep.

ALOYSIUS. *(With a louder whisper, an' a nod to rally on the porch….)* Jeb?! *(JEB looks aroun' suspiciously, then goes to the porch. ALOYSIUS is in JEB'S chair. JEB shoots him a look. ALOYSIUS moves to his own chair. JEB sets. ALOYSIUS continues to whisper as if there was robbers on the property.)* If the lan' can talk, you ever wonder what them onions talk about? *(Beat. ALOYSIUS looks aroun' with paranoia.)* I figger, if they's jus' layin' there day after day after day after day after day … with nothin' better to do than grow a inch er two, why not chat a bit? In there own little onion language, a course.

JEB. 'Course.

ALOYSIUS. What if them sweet little fellas are sayin' bad things about us, an' all?

JEB. 'At's ridiculous. *(Beat.)* 'Sides, it don't matter if onions are shootin' their mouths off about me. *(Beat.)* They don't know me good er nothin'. I mean, what fool is gonna take an onion's word over mine?

ALOYSIUS. I seen you an' Papa curse at them onions once a day er so. Maybe they's feelin's is hurt, so they put their little hangin' heads together an' decided to contaminate the soil when they's picked. Then the dirt's hopin' we change to peanuts er radishes er sugar beets ... somepin less thin-skinned an' sensitive. An' if we don't listen to the dirt, it blows on over to Nebraska in search of sweet peas—er whatever it's cravin'. Kinda like when you gobble down a hot pepper an' yer hollerin' fer a piece a bread to soak up the sting ... er like when I git a hankerin' fer Mama's stuffed art-ee-chokes an' I cain't feel satisfied 'til I take eight er nine of 'em in me ... er like—

JEB. You jabberin' to me 'bout tempermen'al dirt with a picky app-ee-tite?

ALOYSIUS. *(Beat.)* What?

JEB. You's gone to the other side! You's gone to the demon!

ALOYSIUS. Someone's gotta tend to the dirt's needs, er she's gonna up an' leave us.

JEB. Tidwell dirt was fine until 'at wicked vagabond dust started layin' in on 'er, takin' advantage of her hospitality. Oh, 'at dust ain't no lady ... a lady always knows when she ain't been asked to stay fer dessert. See, Aloysius, dirt is diff'ernt than dust.

ALOYSIUS. *(Ignorin' him.)* Uh huh. Mama cain't sleep a wink until the pigs is slopped. So ... I's a sloppin'*!! (ALOYSIUS gits the milk can an' goes offstage to the pig pen.)* SOO-EE! SOO-EE! (*We hear snorts of hungry pigs.*) Jeb? You been so diff'ernt lately. Seems like I don't hardly knows ya. *(JEB kicks a rusty old tin can an' lays his tired sad eyes on the dyin' crop.)* 'Member when we use' ta be so close kin 'at Papa said he needed a butter knife to separate us? Papa is always sayin' poetic stuff like 'at. Never went to school or nothin'. But I hear that kinda thing's in ya. Like a splinter you cain't ever git out.

(The win' roars. The voice of ALOYSIUS fades as JEB picks up a dried-out onion, an' sniffs it. He mumbles to hisself ...)

JEB. Godfersaken smell.

(A smug trail of laughter haunts JEB. He drops the onion as if he has

*seen an' heard the devil hisself. The laughter an' the win' fade
out as ALOYSIUS skips in.)*

ALOYSIUS. ...'Member when we was youngins, an' Mama'd go
inta the berry patch an' fin' us all purply an' sick to our stomachs
from playin' 'at "I can eat a million more berries 'an you!" game?
(*Sees JEB holdin' a look of horror.*) Jeb ... you look like ya seen a
dead man dancin'.

JEB. *(Shook up.)* Jus' the win'.

ALOYSIUS. An' member Mama's fingers looked so big, like
pillas, grabbin' the stickers offa us at the end of a day of good
pickin'....

JEB. Them big fat white fingers a hers.... Yep. 'At's when we
use' ta pick fer fun, fer pies an' jam.

ALOYSIUS. Mama's fingers ain't fat. They's like ... like ...
angel's fingers. Like 'at.

JEB. They were fat. Fat like the onions they smelled of. Stinkin'
from ever' pore....

ALOYSIUS. Quit Jeb! *(Beat.)* Tell me why, why you say them
awful things?

JEB. You gotta grow up sometime, Aloysius. See things fer what
they is. Even if they's ugly. Then you'll be strong. You'll be a man.

ALOYSIUS. Then I don't ever wanna be a man. Ever.

(Beat. JEB changes his tactic.)

JEB. 'Member ol' man Crockett? 'At crazy coot 'at lives over
yonder on Peabody Pond? The one who wears 'at sorta ... colorful
scarf aroun' his neck?

ALOYSIUS. Yer gonna show me ugly stuff, ain't ya?

JEB. What I'm about to tell ya is gonna scare all 'at lilly-liver
outta you. Now dadgummit, concentrate! *(Beat.)* Fifty years ago,
Crockett was a boy jus' like you, healthy an' fulla piss an' vinegar.
The gals in town use' ta cry when he'd walk by on accounta he was so
purty. Then one day, the Powder sisters, famous fer they's headlights
an' they's pree-cision in the hootchie-cootchie, well, they made a bet
to see which a them could git Crockett to propose. Them gals did

ever'thin' shy of honey-fuckin' him, an' do you know what he said? Crockett actually said, *(In a del-ee-cate like voice.)* "They's on'y one woman in my life, an' 'at's my mama." An' to this day, no woman has set foot inside Crockett territory. His mama passed about ten years ago, an' there he sits, alone on his porch, with no visitors— 'cept Father Weary who prays with 'im daily, tryin' to show 'im the way I guess. Some say Crockett comes to town on occasion, an' he'll be wearin' one a his mama's funny hats. An' word has it that ever sence he turned away the sight of a beautiful woman, he ain't been able to hunt, er fish, piss fer distance er nothin'!

ALOYSIUS. Don't tell me no more! It's so ugly!

JEB. *(Smiles.)* You really think so?

ALOYSIUS. Goodness gracious, no more a this Mother Machree! Poor ol' Crockett must miss his mama somepin terr'ble. Afterall, headlights ain't no substitute fer love, brother. I should take 'im a piece a Mama's pee-can pie. Bet no one ever brings 'im pie....

JEB. He don' need no pie! He needs the love of a good woman, goddammit!

ALOYSIUS. *(Beat.)* How'd his mama die, Jeb?

JEB. What'd I jus' finish 'splainin'?

ALOYSIUS. Why Mr. Crockett wears 'at sorta colorful scarf? *(Beat.)* Mama don' even have a winter coat.

JEB. I was showin' you how ugly life can git if you don't use what God give ya.

ALOYSIUS. 'At was a truly upsettin' story.

JEB. I cain't put more sugar on it than 'at.

ALOYSIUS. Well, why don't you jus' drown some kittens in a barrel, fer Chris'sake?

JEB. Would I put you through somepin fer no good reason?

ALOYSIUS. One time, you punched me in the nose ... no damn good reason.

JEB. Y'all didn' do nothin'?

ALOYSIUS. I was jus' walkin'.

JEB. Jus' walkin'?

ALOYSIUS. I was jus' walkin', sorta like 'is.

(ALOYSIUS limps in his most annoyin' way.)

JEB. 'Xactly.

ALOYSIUS. 'Cause sometimes I drag one foot to the side, like 'is.

JEB. I knows you walk like 'at! Hell, I'm yer brother, I see ya ever' damn day!

ALOYSIUS. You really think of me like a brother, Jeb?

JEB. Y'are my brother!

ALOYSIUS. Yeah, but it's nice 'at ya think a me like one.

(Lookin' at him adoringly, ALOYSIUS picks him up with a big hug.)

JEB. Aw, criminy, cut that out! How're you ever gonna git a woman with 'at personality?

ALOYSIUS. I don't wanna woman.

(The cardinal sin of a Tidwell.)

JEB. What did you say?

ALOYSIUS. I don't wanna woman. (*Shoutin' to the crop.*) I DON'T WANNA WOMAN! I DON'T WANNA WO—!

JEB. *(Coverin' his little brother's mouth.)* Shush up! You'll curse us fer sure, an' we'll never git a woman! *(ALOYSIUS giggles at JEB'S fun game.)* I'll kill ya! I'll slit yer throat right'chere!

(ALOYSIUS becomes silent. JEB lets him go. Beat. ALOYSIUS smiles with optimism.)

ALOYSIUS. We still got Mama.

JEB. *(Beat; softly.)* Yeah, Mama. *(Beat; slaps hisself hard.)* Damn skeeter!

ALOYSIUS. Kill it Jeb, kill the Son of a B! HAH! *(JEB chases the mosquito aroun', slappin' at it wildly. ALOYSIUS follows like a jumpin' bean. The bug leaves an' they is once again alone, in silence. Beat. ALOYSIUS creeps to listen at the door, then creeps to his porch chair.)* I think Mama fin'lly settled inta her mornin' nap.

JEB. Aloysius

ALOYSIUS. SSSSSSSSHHHHH!

JEB. *(Whisperin'.)* Aloysius … one day, Mama's gonna be too old fer us.

ALOYSIUS. I don't wanna talk about it.

JEB. *(Pullin' a piece of candy from his pocket.)* Here, have a butterscotch.

ALOYSIUS. Golly, thankee. An' they's no pocket stuck to it er nothin'.

(ALOYSIUS del-ee-cately licks the candy. JEB sits back an' pulls out a mouth harp, strokin' one slow, depressin' chord at a time, in a dirge-like fashion. ALOYSIUS puts the candy in his pocket an' gits his spoons out to join his brother.
He del-ee-cately clicks one "ching" after JEB'S dronin' chord. Fin'lly, ALOYSIUS starts clangin' away as if he is at a jamboree—suddenly, we hear the honkin' of a car horn. ALOYSIUS an' his spoons go flyin' at the noise, as he stan's on his porch chair, searchin' fer intruders.)

ALOYSIUS. WHO'S 'AT!

JEB. Cain't see 'em fer the dust they's raisin'.

ALOYSIUS. *(Imitatin' JEB.)* I'LL KILL 'EM! I'LL SLIT THEIR THROATS RIGHT'CHERE!!

(He smiles for JEB'S approval.)

JEB. Well, I'll be a monkey's uncle. If it ain't Penny Bumpinmeyer crawlin' on back to me like a moth to a flame. I knew she couldn' stay away. I am gonna make her beg, like a dog at a barbecue.

ALOYSIUS. Who's 'at boy with her?

JEB. Her kid sister, Clementine … Clementine Ruth.

ALOYSIUS. No kiddin'? She won 'at dirt clod pitchin' contest at the county fair las' year.

(JEB spits in his han's, then runs his fingers through his hair to primp.)

JEB. If Penny thinks 'at she can jus' prance back inta my corral, boppin' herself aroun', she's got another thing comin'! Watch 'is....

(PENNY BUMPINMEYER, 20, in a "dress-to-kill" ensemble struts in with her kid sister CLEMENTINE, 17, who is wearin' overalls an' a hat. JEB melts as PENNY slinks past him.)

JEB. Hey Penny. *(PENNY don't say nothin'. Instead, she poses like a Greek statue, waitin' to be admired. JEB coolly approaches her.)* Hey Penny.
PENNY. Ya miss me, cowboy?
JEB. *(Droppin' to his knees, he clutches PENNY.)* Like my Appaloosa misses lickin' his salt block.
PENNY. You rascal.
ALOYSIUS. *(Proudly to CLEMENTINE.)* 'At's my brother.
CLEMENTINE. Uh huh.
JEB. Penny, why ya comin' back to me on yer knees?

(JEB realizes he is on his knees. He rises nonchalantly.)

PENNY. Came to say "Good-bye," Jeb.
JEB. In a pig's ass!
PENNY. It's true. We're leavin'. Papa, Clementine an' I are leavin' Hooker. We're goin' to Califor-nee to pick. They got ever'thin' under the sun out there. A regular smorgasbord to feast on.
CLEMENTINE. They got magic dirt.
PENNY. Them people out west, they's livin' high an' mighty, an' I'm a-gonna grab me a piece a that pie, 'fore it's all et up. Papa gimme the car to say my good-byes. So … good-bye y'all.
CLEMENTINE. Bye.

(PENNY grabs CLEMENTINE by the han', an' starts fer the car. ALOYSIUS jumps in front of them an' then nonchalantly asks ...)

ALOYSIUS. Y'all jus' givin' up?
PENNY. Our farm is practic'lly undergroun'. Inches an' inches of 'at rotten dust layin' over our crops like a brown blanket ... suffocatin' us like we was nothin'. You boys ain't no strangers to it.

Jus' look out there. What're ya pickin'? A fiel' fulla skeletons, cryin' 'cause they cain't fill our plates?

CLEMENTINE. It's so sad.

ALOYSIUS. (*Takin' it personally.*) Y'ALL GO ON THEN! WE DON'T WANT Y'ALL HERE! Y'ALL DON'T KNOW NOTHIN! NOTHIN'!

JEB. ALOYSIUS! SHUT YER MOUTH! She can go if she wants to. *(Beat. PENNY starts to go. JEB hollers ...)* I FEEL SICK IN MY BELLY! I got a bad feelin'. (*The girls stop. ALOYSIUS approaches JEB to comfort him. JEB pushes him away an' motions PENNY over with a nonchalant jerk of the head, but now CLEMENTINE approaches. JEB shakes his head "No," then motions again to PENNY. PENNY approaches an' rubs his belly.)* Penny? Tell me one thing…. How many farms did you visit to kiss goodbye?

PENNY. No need to upset yerself, Jeb.

JEB. Tex?! Billy?! CARL?! *(PENNY gives him a slap in the belly, then goes to set with CLEMENTINE on the porch. They shoot the breeze as if JEB'S tantrum weren't nothin'.)* WHO ELSE?! Who else has been lickin' yer pork chops 'at you flaunt aroun' like the meat hangin' in MaGuire's winda? I knew you was trouble the first time I laid eyes on you … in Kind'rgarden. You was always usin' yer feminine wiles to git boys to build you them castles in the san'box…. Playin' hopscotch with them sexy ways of yers, winkin' at me 'fore you threw yer marker, tryin' to distract me from the game! NOTHIN'S CHANGED! I went through elemen'ary school an' on'y learned one thing … 'at Penny Bumpinmeyer collec's boys with a lick an' a promise. I ain't no such fool, no siree! I's a regular cake-eater, a drugstore cowboy, an' I don't wanna be tied down to no woman! An' when you leave, I'll be happy as a pig in clover! So make quick like a bunny an' pick in someone else's fiel'!

(Beat. PENNY smiles. CLEMENTINE giggles. ALOYSIUS has a look of worry.)

PENNY. Good Lord, Jeb, yer in love with me.

JEB. Does 'at sound like love to you?

ALOYSIUS and CLEMENTINE. Yep.

JEB. *(Pointin' to each of them.)* Well ... I's sick of you, an' I's sick of you, an' I's sick of you! Now git off my lan', all a-you's! I'S SICK OF ALL OF Y'ALL! NOW GIT!

(They don't move. Long beat.)

CLEMENTINE. *(To PENNY:)* He's cotton crazy, he is.

JEB. *(A pause.)* Awright, you can stay. But I dee-mand ree-spect! It's plain crucial to my well bein'.

PENNY. An' all these years, I thought you was jus' pitchin' hay ... but you meant it, didn't ya?

JEB. Yes. What? I mean, no! What? Goddammit, there, yer doin' it again! Usin' 'at confusin' woman talk on me!

ALOYSIUS. Seems clear as day to me, Jeb.

JEB. Somebody speakin' to you, boy?!

ALOYSIUS. But you tol' me you loved Penny more 'an Sugar Rump. *(To the gals.)* 'At's his prize sow.

(JEB looks at ALOYSIUS as if he has stripped 'im naked. JEB falls to the floor, clutches his head an' hollers in horror...)

JEB. AAAAAAAHHHHHHH!!!!

(JEB freezes with a pained expression. Silence. Long beat. The others look at JEB as if he is a right interestin' statue.)

CLEMENTINE. I think he's havin' hisself a heart ee-tack.

ALOYSIUS. Nah. He'll sit like 'at fer hours if you suprise him real good. I's the on'y one 'at can lif' the curse ... keep him from squanderin' his whole day. Somepin on'y kin would know.

PENNY. Bet I can unfreeze him.

ALOYSIUS. Ha ha ha. I sure do git a kick outta you, Penelope Bumpinmeyer.

CLEMENTINE. You don't know my sister, Aloysius. She can bring a man back from the dead.

(PENNY crawls to her prey. CLEMENTINE crawls behin' her,

studyin' her technique. PENNY whispers in JEB'S ear ...)

PENNY. Wanna know what I'm wearin' underneath 'is dress?
JEB. (*Unfreezin'.)* Yep.
CLEMENTINE. See. Told ya.
ALOYSIUS. 'At's one way a-goin' about it, I guess.
JEB. *(Eyein' PENNY'S neck.)* What in tarnation is 'at?
PENNY. What's what, darlin'?
JEB. On yer neck? What's 'at say on yer neck?!
PENNY. Oh, one of my good-byes gotta little hot to trot, an'
sucked 'is initials inta me.
CLEMENTINE. *(Chucklin'.)* Johnnie Elbert. He 'bout swallowed
'er up like a trout does a night crawler.
ALOYSIUS. Them trout can be brutal.

*(The three look at ALOYSIUS due to the randomness of this remark.
ALOYSIUS traces the bark on the tree to look busy. Beat. JEB
picks up where he left off ...)*

JEB. Are you standin' on my porch, on my lan', in my—
ALOYSIUS. Jeb, it's Papa's lan'.
JEB. Little brother, let me handle the women folk! *(Back to
PENNY.)* Are you standin' on my porch, on my lan', in my great state
a Oklahoma, tellin' me Johnnie Elbert Miller gave you a love bite?
An' you stood still long enough fer him to spell? 'At Herkimer
Jerkimer wouldn' know how to write S.O.S.!
ALOYSIUS. *(Supportin' his brother.)* Herkimer Jerkimer!
JEB. What do you think you are, a cow in need of brandin'?
Christ allmighty, why don't ya jus' git my gun outta the barn an' shoot
me already!
PENNY. There you go again, rantin' an' ravin' like you own me
er somepin! No man owns me! I, am a modern woman. I do what I
want, when I want, with who I want, suckin' er not.
JEB. 'At's jus' fine, 'cause I don't wanna suck on you's anyways!
PENNY. (*Grabbin' JEB'S shirt.)* Ooohh, I jus' hate you!
JEB. An' I hate you more!
PENNY. *(Kissin' JEB lustfully.)* Cowboy, you are harder than

Chinese arithmetic.

> JEB. *(Kissin' her back lustfully.)* Wanna go to the barn?
> PENNY. More than a cat in a rainstorm!

(PENNY pulls out a flask of alkee-hol. JEB picks her up. PENNY'S legs are wrapped aroun' him as he struggles to carry PENNY. ALOYSIUS hollers ...)

> ALOYSIUS. Gee, Penny, yer lookin' real fat!

(JEB puts her down, an' holds his back in pain. PENNY approaches ALOYSIUS as if she is about to square off when JEB pulls her away.)

> JEB. Jus' walk baby, walk.

(JEB an' PENNY exit to the barn. ALOYSIUS an' CLEMENTINE is left alone in an awkward silence. ALOYSIUS turns aroun' to fin' CLEMENTINE a-settin' on the porch with a lustful smile. He looks down, embarrassed. He picks at his clothes, whistles, anythin' to fill the silence.)

> CLEMENTINE. What'cha doin', Aloysius?
> ALOYSIUS. This minute?
> CLEMENTINE. Uh huh.
> ALOYSIUS. Nothin'.
> CLEMENTINE. *(Chucklin'.)* You say the most clever things!
> ALOYSIUS. Do not.
> CLEMENTINE. Aloysius?
> ALOYSIUS. Yep.
> CLEMENTINE. You like pickin'?
> ALOYSIUS. Is what I am.
> CLEMENTINE. But do ya like it?
> ALOYSIUS. Never thought about it.
> CLEMENTINE. Try it.

(ALOYSIUS becomes statue-like with his mouth open, in thought er

somepin, as CLEMENTINE adores him. ALOYSIUS begins to pantomime stunted pickin' motions as if he is a cat havin' a dream. CLEMENTINE bats her eyelashes on his cheek. ALOYSIUS jumps fer the high heavens.)

ALOYSIUS. HEY! You tryin' to scare the bejesus outta me?

CLEMENTINE. Silly, I was jus' givin' you's a butterfly kiss. Didn't ya like it?

ALOYSIUS. Don't ever pull a crazy stunt like 'at again! You know I ain't as much the ladies' man as my brother. Mama says I's what ya call "genuine un-tilled soil."

CLEMENTINE. No kiddin'.

ALOYSIUS. *(Lookin' toward barn.)* They sure been gone a long time, don'tcha think? We gotta git pickin'...'sides, what's there to do in 'at ol' barn anyhow?

CLEMENTINE. They ain't playin' "hide the peanut," Aloysius.

ALOYSIUS. 'Course not. 'At's a dumb game.

CLEMENTINE. Come sit down an' talk nice to me. *(Pattin' the chair.)* Right'chere. *(ALOYSIUS eyes the doorway to make sure his mama ain't lookin'. Then he reluctantly sets next to CLEMENTINE on the milk can. An uncomfortable silence. CLEMENTINE unbuttons her blouse an' fans herself with affectation.)* Sure is hot.

ALOYSIUS. Had a dog named Clementine once. He ran away, though. Now we don't got him no more. On accounta he's gone an' all....

CLEMENTINE. *(Her best sexy comeback.)* Woof!

ALOYSIUS. Now we got Stump. He would never run away. He ain't no trouble. Watch. *(Points to STUMP.)* SIT BOY! STAY! *(Back to CLEMENTINE.)* See?

(CLEMENTINE crinkles her forehead at the sight of the dead dog. She shakes off that gruesome pi'ture, an' seductively lets her hair down. ALOYSIUS tries to distract her by drawin' in the dust.)

ALOYSIUS. Drew you a flower.

CLEMENTINE. In the dust?

ALOYSIUS. *(Defensively.)* DIRT!... From my boots. I'd draw

Mama flowers, but she's allergic.

CLEMENTINE. 'At's sweet.

ALOYSIUS. Clementine. What's the name of 'at song, it goes ... *(Singin' horribly.)* "Oh my darlin', Oh my darlin', Oh my darlin' Clementine...."

CLEMENTINE. Please, don't go on....

ALOYSIUS. Okey Dokey.

CLEMENTINE. *(Tryin' to unbutton his shirt.)* Maybe you could give me somepin to 'member you by, like Jeb is givin' Penny in the barn?

(ALOYSIUS thinks for a moment, then pulls out his butterscotch candy, picks the pocket off it, licks it clean, an' offers it to her.)

CLEMENTINE. I wasn't talkin' about 'at kind of candy, Aloysius.

ALOYSIUS. *(Shrugs, unwraps butterscotch an' sucks on it.)* Mmmm.

CLEMENTINE. Mmmmm....

(Frightened by the look in CLEMENTINE'S eye, ALOYSIUS rises, then jumps when he hears MAMA. CLEMENTINE falls outta her chair.)

ALOYSIUS. *(Straightenin' hisself.)* Yes, Mama! T'ain't nobody! Jus' two a Kelsey's billygoats got out an' I'm tryin' to ... corral 'em an' quiet 'em down. *(CLEMENTINE stan's on the porch chair an' teases him with goat sounds.)* GIT NOW! GIT! *(Whisperin'.)* Mama'll kill you if she finds you here!

CLEMENTINE. Don'tcha like girls, Aloysius?

ALOYSIUS. Quit! Yer givin' me the duckbumps. 'Sides, Mama says I gots to stay away from the evil 'at's under most of the skirts in 'is town— 'Cept fer Widow Dadendower, Mama says at eighty-four, she ain't got no evil left.

CLEMENTINE. An' what's yer mama think I's gonna do to you, Aloysius?

ALOYSIUS. Mama says it starts out right innocent enough, with smilin', gigglin', pawin', but then the monster creeps out an' the nightmare begins!

CLEMENTINE. (*In awe.*) An' then?

ALOYSIUS. Mama says it's got teeth! Y'all will clamp down on me an' I'll never git away!

CLEMENTINE. Oh boy! Aloysius, did ya ever think that makin' love could be so dramatic? 'At's what they do in the big city, you know, "Drama!" They's "women" there. They knows what they want an' they talk about it real fancy-like, which always makes it better than it really is. Like in the movin' pi'tures. Like 'at.

ALOYSIUS. (*Deflectin'.*) They sure been gone a long time.

CLEMENTINE. It's got teeth!... Huh, if 'at don't beat all! My mama musta lef' 'at part out.

ALOYSIUS. Yer mama?

CLEMENTINE. Betty Bumpinmeyer—GOD REST MY MAMA'S SWEET NAME! AMEN! She said when you's ripe, the crop'll wink an' the angel of the fiel' will lif' you up outta this dirt an' take you where it's clean—keep ya from draggin' filth through the house an' back again. An' if the love is pure, the onions'll rise up, 'steada buryin' they's heads outta shame. 'At's the day we'll be fat an' happy, she said. An' my trouble won't come again. 'At's when we'll all be saved.

ALOYSIUS. (*Sadly.*) Yer mama *said.* She *said?*

CLEMENTINE. Them were her last words ... like a secret map to a treasure. Special instructions she whispered inta Penny's ear a'fore she passed.

ALOYSIUS. You let yer mama go?

CLEMENTINE. No, I cain't say I did. Penny said she was so happy to see me when I was born, she died jus' from smilin'. So I never had a chance. An' they's somepin in 'at.

(*Beat. ALOYSIUS almost cries at this. He deflects an' wipes his eyes.*)

ALOYSIUS. They sure been gone a long time.

CLEMENTINE. ... I'm a-goin' to Califor-nee, what'cha say a'fore I go, you make me fat ... an happy.

ALOYSIUS. Huh?

CLEMENTINE. Aloysius, I wanna be a woman! *(CLEMENTINE fiercely grabs ALOYSIUS an' kisses him. He stiffens with fear, then faints outta sheer fright. She stan's over him with accomplishment.)* The power of modern love! Ain't it grand!

(JEB an' PENNY come on back in a fight, half-dressed, an' half-looped.)

PENNY. Yer as stubborn as a mule, Jeb Tidwell!

JEB. Jus' ferget it! Ferget I ever said it! Go back to Carl! You like him better!

PENNY. I cain't marry you right now, Jeb!

JEB. Good, 'cause I don't wanna marry you anyways!

CLEMENTINE. Yer gittin' married?

PENNY and JEB. HELL NO!

CLEMENTINE. Jinxies.

PENNY. You jus' wanna pee on me, like a dog markin' his territory, an' then put me in a glass case, 'at on'y you have the key to.

JEB. You say 'at like it's a bad thing.

CLEMENTINE. *(To an unconscious ALOYSIUS.)* They's so in love!

ALOYSIUS. *(Mumbles somepin.)* IiiiillluuvvvuuumammmmmaIddoo.

JEB. What'sa matter'th 'im?

CLEMENTINE. He got hisself stung.

JEB. What? He ain't swollen er nothin'.

CLEMENTINE. He's in his "passion flight."

JEB. What in the devil has ya done to him?

ALOYSIUS. *(Thawin'.)* Where am I? Jeb? Jeb. I was havin' this won'erful dream, you an' me an' Mama was there. No Papa at all. An' Mama was rockin', in her chair, the fire behin' her, with her big lovin' han's makin' puppets on the wall jus' to pass the dark night of rain tap tap tappin' on the winda....

JEB. 'At was a dream awright.

PENNY. *(Tryin' to git his attention.)* Jeb, I's a-goin'! I's a-goin' to Califor-nee!

JEB. I knows.

ALOYSIUS. … An' there was plen'y a healthy crop, far as the eye could see….

PENNY. I's a-walkin' to the car now.

CLEMENTINE. We's a-walkin'!

ALOYSIUS. … An' Mama made this one huge shadow of a red-bellied woodpecker—

JEB. Shush up Aloysius! Shush up all of y'alls! I gotta think! Think! Think think think!

CLEMENTINE. He's gonna hurt hisself.

JEB. Penny, I'm gonna ask you one more time. Now, I knows you got big plans fer yer life an' all, but godammit, if you don't marry me I mise well dig myself a hole an' choke right along with them onions, stinkin' an' smellin' somepin awful. Marry me, Penny. We can ask Father weary to bring 'at bible a his on over to the barn an' seal us like … like—

CLEMENTINE. Like Anthony an' Cleopatra.

ALOYSIUS. Like peanut butter an' jelly. Like 'at. 'At's good sealin'.

JEB. Penny … babydoll….

PENNY. I cain't. I cain't be yer … yer jelly, Jeb.

JEB. I'll take care of ya, even if I has to git myself a job shovelin' manure.

ALOYSIUS. Y'already do 'at, Jeb. Fer nothin'.

PENNY. I'm leavin' Hooker behin', cowboy. I'm a-gonna start over.

JEB. Then I'll come with y'all.

ALOYSIUS. You cain't do that.

JEB. We'll come to Califor-nee. Aloysius an' me. A new life.

ALOYSIUS. You cain't leave! We cain't leave! What about Mama an' Papa, an' Stump?!

JEB. Shush up, Aloysius! I'm talkin'. Now Penny—

ALOYSIUS. I will not shush up! We ain't leavin'. We's stuck to the groun' here, jus' like crop. We cain't leave! An' you cain't up an' yank us!

JEB. Goddammit, Aloysius!

(JEB shoves ALOYSIUS. Beat.)

ALOYSIUS. EVIL WOMEN!

JEB. I'm still yer older brother—

ALOYSIUS. I ain't gonna let you do this! Yer crazy! Yer crazy with the fever ... the nasty fever them Bumpinmeyer's have been handin' down sence Jesus was born, an' I ain't budgin' fer no good time, no siree!

JEB. *(Grabbin' ALOYSIUS.)* Don't you git it!? Dust is comin' anyways! We gotta git outta this damn town! It's gonna starve us to death!

ALOYSIUS. 'At loosey goosey has turned yer head all inta mush. You don't know what yer sayin'! We're gonna be fine. You, me, Papa, an' Mama is gonna be fine, right'chere, seein' the crop through! *(Chantin'.)* You, me, Papa an' Mama. You, me, Papa an' Mama...

JEB. Mama? Mama?!

ALOYSIUS. Mama says a little dust never hurt nobody. Mama knows.

JEB. Mama don't know nothin'!

ALOYSIUS. You take 'at back!

JEB. Mama don't know nothin' CUZ MAMA'S DEAD GOD-DAMMIT! DO YOU HEAR ME?! MAMA IS DEAD!

(JEB shoves ALOYSIUS to the groun'. ALOYSIUS stays still. Long beat.)

PENNY. Jeb ... think about what yer sayin'.

JEB. I'm sayin' my mama passed. I'm sayin' it. Three long days ago, she left us.

ALOYSIUS. Yer a liar, Jeb Tidwell! A liar! *(Callin' to MAMA, panicked.)* Mama! Mama!

PENNY. Jeb, if yer jokin', 'at is the cruelest thing I ever did hear.

ALOYSIUS. *(Goes to doorway.)* Mama? Mama?

(ALOYSIUS backs away slowly, too scairt to go inside.)

CLEMENTINE. *(To JEB.)* I saw Mrs. Tidwell in church on Sund'y, passin' out her pee-can pie with a smile an' a good word. She was fine.

PENNY. Dammit, Jeb, if yer tryin' to tie me here with 'at nonsense, you cut it out right now! Yer gonna kill 'im!

(ALOYSIUS goes to MAMA'S dress on the line an' embraces it.)

ALOYSIUS. Mama … Mama….
CLEMENTINE. Aloysius! He's jus' playin'. Ain't ya Jeb?
PENNY. Ain't ya?

(ALOYSIUS brings dress to the edge of the fiel' an' curls into a fetal position.)

JEB. Playin'? Aloysius, am I playin'? Let's see now … Mama's lyin' up there in yer room, face down at the end of yer bed like a paintin', prayin' fer God to take 'er away from 'at selfish plot of hell out the winda…. Prayin' 'at her life would be worth more 'an a couple boxes of onions an' two sons survivin' by eatin' the food outta her mouth. Even after she passed, she's still starin' at ya, lookin' after ya. An' not one of us, not one of us had the decency to move her. *(JEB begins to weep.)* We "men," Papa an' me, we jus' lef' her kneelin' there, stiff with a worried smile, an' cold as the storm 'at blew in with the sand in its pocket. We didn't wanna carry her, the weight of her, down the stairs even. We didn't wanna interrupt the harvest … we might lose a minute of pickin', jus' leave her be. An' you, all's you can do is warsh the clothes 'at layed on her when this dusty old farm took her. Her best Sund'y dress! *(JEB grabs the dress that ALOYSIUS clutches, an' shakes it. Dust scatters.)* … DUST! 'At's what Mama is now! DUST!

(JEB takes the dress an' shows it to the girls as if it were a bird that had broken its neck on the winda. He looks to the girls fer hope, fer words to ease the pain, fer acknowledgment.)

PENNY. I'm so sorry, Jeb. I know you loved your Mama.
CLEMENTINE. She was an angel, that Erma Tidwell. T'ain't no lie.
JEB. Jus' like ever'thin' aroun' us … ever'thing we worked fer

all our lives.

ALOYSIUS. *(Beat. Cryin'.)* Yer drunk. You don't know what yer sayin'.

(Droppin' to the groun', JEB picks up a han'ful of dirt. As it sifts through his fingers, he hopelessly speaks to the demon.)

JEB. No crop, no fam'ly, nothin' but you, black murderer! "Dust we are an' dust we shall return!"

ALOYSIUS. Papa's gonna come back an' whoop ya fer this! Whoop ya good!

JEB. Papa ain't comin' back! Papa took the car, took what's left a the food, an' is prob'ly half way through Texas by now, ya fool! He don't want us, he don't need us, an' he sure as hell don't miss us! *(Beat. Reality leaves JEB as he slides into "PAPA" for a moment—his voice harsh an' gruff ...)* Yer a good fer nothin', Aloysius! Yer a stupid, worthless, crybaby, who ain't gonna amount to nothin'! NOTHIN'!

(JEB raises his han' to strike ALOYSIUS, as a dust cloud raises with the clamor.)

ALOYSIUS. Don't hit me! Papa, please don't hit me!
PENNY. Jeb! You crazy?!

(JEB snaps out of it, realizes what he is doin', an' lowers his han'. CLEMENTINE holds ALOYSIUS like a baby.)

ALOYSIUS. *(Cryin'.)* Don't hit me, Papa. I didn't mean to upset you. I didn't mean to, I swear. I won't do it again. I promise. Papa? Papa? I'll fetch yer whiskey. I'll fetch yer whiskey.

CLEMENTINE. You don't fetch nobody nothin'.
JEB. *(Reaches for ALOYSIUS.)* Aloysius—
CLEMENTINE. Don't you touch him!

(JEB walks to the edge of the fiel' with a look of doom. PENNY approaches, an' puts a han' on JEB'S shoulder. Long beat.)

PENNY. Why didn't you tell me about yer Mama?
JEB. Would it have made a diff'ernce? Dust is still comin'.
PENNY. They's always hope.
JEB. Hope?
(Beat. CLEMENTINE sings the lullaby, "Hush little baby," to soothe ALOYSIUS.)

CLEMENTINE. (*Singin'*)
"Hush little baby don't say a word,
Mama's gonna buy you a mockin'bird..."
ALOYSIUS. (*Joinin' in singin'.*)
"An' if 'at mockin'bird don't sing,
Mama's gonna buy you a diamond ring."
JEB. Aloysius, go inside. It's lunchtime an'... an'... an' Mama's callin' ya.

(ALOYSIUS stops cryin', an' rises as if the clouds have lifted. He takes the dress, goes to the door an' talks to MAMA with a smile.)

ALOYSIUS. Mama? I finished the chores like you asked me to. Mmmmm ... you been cookin' up somepin special? Ooooh, Jeb is gonna like 'at. Let me help you with 'at heavy skillet.

(JEB, PENNY an' CLEMENTINE stare out inta the bleak black fiel'. We hear the eerie sound of a dust storm approachin'. Lights fade to black--blacker than you ever seen. Ever.)

Intermission

ACT II

Scene 1

(1935. A scorchin' hot October afternoon in the fiel' of the abandoned Tidwell Farm. We cain't see the farmhouse no mores, jus' the tired ol' body of DUSTY, alone, in a beam of sunlight, a-settin' on an ol' fruit crate. He is plunkin' the banjo, an' singin' the Woody Guthrie tune, "Do Re Mi."* The Tidwells have gone West. DUSTY sings a facetious farewell ...)

DUSTY.
"Wellll, lotsa folks back east, they say, is leavin' home ever'day,
An' beatin' the hot ol' dusty way to the California line,
Across the desert sands they'd roll, gettin' the ol' Dustbowl,
They think they're goin' to a sugar bowl, but here is what they find,
The police at the port of entry say,
You're number fourteen thousand fer today....'

Oh, if you ain't got the Do Re Mi, folks,
If you ain't got the Do Re Mi,
You better go back to beautiful Texas, Oklahoma, Kansas,
   Georgia, Tennessee...
California's a garden of Eden, a paradise to live in or see,
But believe it or not, you won't find it so hot, if you ain't got the Do
   Re Mi."

(DUSTY chuckles, then turns aroun' as his sunlight fades. He begins plunkin' a moody sad song, "Leavin' Blues,* softly underscorin' the followin' monologues. The next two locations are shown as if DUSTY was lookin' in on 'em ... followin' 'em.

---

*See page three for information on obtaining permission to use these songs.

*JEB, ALOYSIUS, PENNY, an' CLEMENTINE enter in a dim light to
form a tableau, freezin' in diff'ernt poses. The BROTHERS loca-
tion is Route 66, on the side of the road, hitchin' a ride to Califor-nee. The SISTERS are in the Imperial Valley migrant camp,
Califor-nee. The two locations of the road an' the camp are si-
multaneous as the boys overlap the girls' monologues. The beam
of sunlight shines bright on the actor speakin', a course. PENNY
stan's with an unlit cigarette, her fingers del-ee-cately liftin' her
dress above her knee. CLEMENTINE is on her knees listenin' to
the earth below her. ALOYSIUS stan's in the form of a cross,
wearin' his hat. JEB sets on a beat-up suitcase with an onion, an'
his thumb out hitchin'. All are still as frogs in mud. JEB un-
freezes an' begins.)*

JEB. *(To onion.)* You ol' dried up, sour, enemy of the eyes!
T'ain't got enough juice fer a thirsty man to squeeze outta ya on the
side of the road. Hun'erd an' one awful blisterin' heat bangin' down
on my head ever' day, an' still I carry you on my back like yer gonna
squirt some kinda oil on my joints an' quench me ... save me, er
somepin. Might as well git blood from a turnip, crops from them
black fiel's, or hope from a road 'at's seen more death than a war.
Foolish talk. An' what's worse, is I got you fer my good luck charm.
Somepin wrong there. Somepin wrong. *(Beat.)* But if you think I's
gonna shrivel up an' die like the rest of yer selfish, skinny little
friends, you got another thing comin'! Yessir, 'cause, I'll wrap my
han's aroun' anythin' to git my lan' back. Grapes, peaches, lettuce,
it's all the same to me. Know what else? They's got manners. They
ain't nothin' like the likes of y'all. They don't feel the need to leave
their smell on ya fer markin', markin' like you owns the han's 'at
killed ya. Manners. Somepin y'all better learn if ya wanna live in this
world of con-see-quence an' mishap. Oh, but you don't wanna live, do
ya? Y'all is about dyin', dyin' 'fore you say a word to the fella 'at
spent more time tendin' to you than his own children. 'At's sweet. As
sweet as you git. *(Beat.)* I'm talkin' to an onion. *(Lookin' to heaven.)*
Damn you Mama, fer not pumpin' me fulla sense. Instead, ya gimme
some a that silly 'at Aloysius speaks from every pitiful pore. People
gonna talk. They's gonna say, "Who was 'at Jeb Tidwell? 'At crazy ...

good lookin'... well-built boy we found dead on Highway Sixty-Six, not a drop a juice in 'im?... Jus' an onion by his side, laughin'." Laughin' like an onion will....

CLEMENTINE. *(Ear to the groun'.)* SSSShhhhh!

JEB. Skin all peelin' back....

CLEMENTINE. I's lis'nin'.

JEB. Vein's poppin' out....

CLEMENTINE. They's a-talkin'....

JEB. Nothin' uglier 'an 'at.

CLEMENTINE. An' I's a-lis'nin'.

JEB. I got me a bucket of onions lef' to take inside me....

CLEMENTINE. *(Listenin', gigglin'.)* Uh huh.

JEB. ...To stop the growlin'.

CLEMENTINE. No kiddin'.

JEB. An' then I's done with 'em,

CLEMENTINE. *(Lookin' into the fiel'.)* This is the place right'chere.

JEB. I's done with them an' 'at god-awful smell....

CLEMENTINE. They's gonna grow fer us...

JEB and CLEMENTINE. Ferever an' ever an' ever....

(JEB freezes as he eyes the onion.)

CLEMENTINE. So's we can eat. So's we can eat buckets full, 'til we make ourselves sick. Oh, wouldn't it be grand to eat like a pig in a river full a slop! Califor-nee! You han'some Lan' o' Plen'y! Bet ya grow the most amazin' crop a girl ever did see. I cain't wait to dip my han's in yer beau-tee-ful furrowed shoulders an' pull me out somepin I can stick to my empty insides. An' rumor has it 'at yer rich, an' 'at's hotter 'an a three dollar pistol! Now they's gonna be other pickers with promises an' wishes, but I'll be true to ya. I'll eat any-thin' 'at comes up, dry er disagreeable. An' I'll sing to ya. See, singin' is like seltzer, it settles ya. An' when you got the blues so bad, I figger if you make some sorta sweet sound, maybe God'll hear ya, an' ya won't disappear. Like when I hear ya hummin' with the crickets after the tractor has dug inta yer back ... tryin' to make it through one more night. Sweet sweet fiel'... you an' me's a lot alike ... we's prayin' fer

a purty face ever' year, 'cause if it don't look good enough to eat, people gonna move on. *(Beat.)* These clumsy ol' han's... couldn' grow
you to purty ... er me. I reckon it don't matter, though ... I was born in
a fiel', an' I s'pose it shows. *(Beat.)* My last fiel' gimme somepin to
prove his devotion. *(She pulls an onion from her pocket.)* But it jus'
made me cry. Maybe you could do better. Although he was awful
sweet to me fer years, he lost his ... potency. It's a shame really ...
seems ever'thin' I touch turns to dust.

    ALOYSIUS. *(Unfreezin'.)* Mama says if ya stan' in the form of a
cross, like 'is....

(CLEMENTINE sings a bit of "Leavin' Blues."*)

    CLEMENTINE. *(Sings.)*
They's "...grasshoppers in my pillow, baby...."
    ALOYSIUS. 'An put yer crop on yer head... *(Takes his hat off to
reveal an onion precariously perched atop his head.)* ... like 'at.
    CLEMENTINE. *(Sings.)*
"Crickets all in my meal...."
    ALOYSIUS. 'An say a little prayer, *(He does, silently.)* like 'at...
    CLEMENTINE. *(Sings.)*
They's "...grasshoppers in my pillow, Mama,"
    ALOYSIUS. Won't change nothin'....
    CLEMENTINE. *(Ear to the earth, addin' her motto.)* It's my
trouble come again.... Sing to me....
    ALOYSIUS. But y'all will feel better...
    CLEMENTINE and ALOYSIUS. Ferever an' ever an' ever....
    ALOYSIUS. An' ever an' ever. An' I do. I do feel better. After-
all, prayer cain't hurt ya none, Mama said. *(He corrects hisself.)* She
says, Mama *says*. *(He bites the onion with fervor.)* Mm. Oniony. Still
the best thing comin' outta the groun' sence sliced bread. *(He looks at
his belly an' flinches.)* Oh, I do love it when it makes my tummy
cramp up like 'at. Sacrifice. Sweet undyin' sacrifice. Givin' my belly
linin' up to the cause! *(Lookin' at the onion.)* Oh ... he knows. He
'preciates my acids a-turnin' aroun' in me like a tater bug through a
cobweb. An' his grateful self will reward his followers with ample

---

onionage. *(Tearin'.)* It's happ'nin'. Ever'time I speaks to him, he chokes me all up like a necktie does a workin' man. He's sad. He didn' do nothin' wrong, an' we jus' up an' lef' him to choke in the sun. Buried alive. Oh, I have betrayed you, little fella. My brother don't understan' nothin'. He's tryin' to keep us apart, hollerin' at me to ferget ya. But I got him plum fooled, 'cause when I's forced to pick ... *(Painful.)* ... p-p-p-otaters, or a-a-artee-chokes, I will be thinkin' a you. Nobody can take 'at away from us. An' you'll see, someday, I'll come home, an' seed y'all up like new, an' maybe with a few gen'le tugs from my beggin' han's, y'all can trust me again. An' when I's tired, an' white with whiskers, I'll pass away, an' they'll bury me....

(He lays hisself down, folds his arms across his chest.)

PENNY. See somepin ya like, Mister?
ALOYSIUS. ... in my best Sund'y jacket....
PENNY. Bet ya do.
ALOYSIUS. ... an' you in my mouth....
PENNY. I'll tell you one thing....
ALOYSIUS. ... squirtin' yer gold down my throat....
PENNY. *(Liftin' her dress higher.)* These legs....
ALOYSIUS. ... so's I can take a piece a you with me.
PENNY. They go on ferever.
PENNY and ALOYSIUS. Ferever an' ever an' ever.

(ALOYSIUS places the onion in his mouth an' freezes.)

PENNY. Like two climbin' vines reachin' fer water. You got clean water? 'Cause I don't do nothin' fer free. An' I know, I know these fiel's take a lot outta a man like you. Times is so hard. *(Beat.)* I lef' my farm. Lef' the lan' my mama was born an' buried on. "Young woman, ol' farm, jus' don't mix." She use' ta say that. But I's jus' happy my mama shut her eyes years ago, 'fore she seen what this place does to ya ... to a woman, to a man. A man who's use' ta ownin' his own lan', sowin' his own seed, pickin' his own crop. It's a terr'ble thing to have yer han's wrapped aroun' a ripe piece a fruit,

pleadin' with ya to bite it open, and then realize, 'at ya has to han' it
over to another man who sells it without blinkin'. Like it didn' mean
nothin'. *(Beat.)* An' that there is the picker's blues. A song you ain't
never played before, up on 'at horse, barkin' at ever'one. You may not
have enough money to buy the bushel, but you got change enough fer
a han'ful, don'tcha? Maybe you'd like to lay yer head against my
chest an' tell me about yer troubles. Papa says I'm a real good list'ner.
Papa says. *(Beat. She lights her cigarette.)* I'm new aroun' here, jus'
like ever'one else, I guess. One diff'rnce. See, I am a dancer. Did ya
know 'at? Even with all those bushels on my back, my feet ain't never
stuck to the groun'. Wil' wil' West. Ya gotta show me a good time, if
yer gonna keep a woman like me. Well, Mr. Gunther, can ya compete
with my fiel'? *(Lookin' to the fiel'.)* 'At raw jagged feelin' I git when I
push my fingers into the dirt, scratchin' the animal ears beneath it.
(Beat.) I sure am hungry... an' cold. You jus' gonna stan' there, er are
you gonna ask me in? *(Takes a last drag off her cigarette, looks back
at her cardboard shack, an' puts out her cigarette. Then to herself,
cynically ...)* Welcome to Californ-ee, Papa. Lan' o' milk an' honey.

*(The beam of light fin's DUSTY again. PENNY, CLEMENTINE,
JEB, an' ALOYSIUS exit in the dark. DUSTY keeps on a-playin'
as he chuckles.)*

SCENE 2

*(1935. A cold foggy November mornin', Imperial Valley Camp, Cali-
for-nee. DUSTY stops plunkin' the banjo as a frosty win' ap-
proaches. He rubs his han's together due to the cold an' smiles.
He rises, tips his hat, an' laughs devilishly as he exits. There are
two weathered cardboard-faced shacks: one belongin' to GRADY
GUNTHER—who ain't never seen— the other to the BUMPIN-
MEYER family. There is a warsh barrel an' a dead fire pit
holdin' a black skillet.*
*A sleepy CLEMENTINE comes outta the BUMPINMEYER shack.
She looks out into the gray, foggy fiel'.)*

CLEMENTINE. Penny? You up? *(Beat. To PAPA inside shack, who ain't never seen.)* I'll fix yer breakfast, Papa. You jus' shave an' git yerself smooth, an' maybe you'll feel up to pickin' today. Californee crop jus' loves to look up an' sees a hansome devil like you pullin' 'em outta they's cradle. *(Beat. She walks to the warsh barrel.)* Looks like Penny's been pickin' by the moonlight in 'at secret lettuce fiel' two miles yonder, workin' herself to tired an' back. But I's here! I's here like a weed! An' I'll sing to ya, 'at song Uncle Clay learn't from 'at fellar in the Lousiana Penetentiary. At'll settle us. *(CLEMENTINE warshes with the barrel water usin' the red kerchief she has wrapped aroun' her neck. She sings, "Leavin Blues,"* to calm herself...)*

They's "grasshoppers in my pillow, baby,
Crickets all in my meal,
They's "grasshoppers in my pillow, Mama,
Crickets all in my meal,"
I got tacks in my shoes, Mama,"
An' they's "stickin' in my heel."
"Rather see my coffin' comin', Mama
Lordy, lordy in my back door,
Rather see my coffin comin', Mama...."

(She stops as she looks inta the frozen fiel'. Beat. She looks at her weathered han's, then down her blouse an' sighs at the sight, then pulls a rusty harmonica from her bosom an' speaks to him.) Oooohhhee, Mister Harmony, yer as cold as a cow's udder on Christmas mornin'. Bet I can change all 'at, han'some. *(She goes to kiss it, then blows a horrible note.)* Aww, yer jus' sayin' 'at. Penny's the purty one. *(She suffers at the sight of her reflection in the harmonica. She blows another awful sound, like slop through an organ, then stops abruptly when a DOG, never seen by the audience, lingers in the fiel' due to the shrillness of the sound.)* Go on you ol' mutt! Git! Cain't two people git a moment alone in all this frost! You ol' wiryhair'd rat-faced belly-fulla-socks! *(She sees an offstage QUINCY KRANSICKLE, an odd lookin' fella, who is out in the fiel', unseen by*

---

*See page three for information on obtaining permission to use this song.

the audience.) Oh! Hey, Quincy! 'At cute little muffin of a doggie a yers been sniffin' the pleasure of the mornin' again. I think the two a you keep lookin' more alike ever'day, yessir. Oooh, he spots ya! *(Through her teeth to the mutt.)* Scoot yer yella self on over to yer Pa, now. *(The DOG scoots.)* See ya Quincy. See ya in the fiel'! *(Cooin', to herself.)* You livin' doll, you.

(PENNY comes outta GRADY GUNTHER'S shack, half-looped.)

    PENNY. Mornin'.
    CLEMENTINE. Papa's hungry!
    PENNY. No kiddin'.
    CLEMENTINE. Papa's hungry an' he wants his breakfast!
    PENNY. Yer doin' jus' fine.
    CLEMENTINE. Ya got dirt on ya.
    PENNY. *(Lookin' at her dress.)* I knows.
    CLEMENTINE. Ya got dirt on yer best dress!
    PENNY. Ya got food, don'tcha'? Bacon, eggs, the likes.
    CLEMENTINE. 'At's a lot a lettuce you been pickin'. 'At poor secret fiel' a yers must be 'bout stripped naked by now.

(PENNY walks defiantly to CLEMENTINE. She raises her skirt, pulls two sausages from her stockin', an' slaps 'em into CLEMENTINE'S han's.)

    PENNY. Cook it up!

(Beat. CLEMENTINE takes the sausages to the fire an' puts 'em in the skillet.)

    CLEMENTINE. Reached over an' you wasn't there this mornin'.
    PENNY. I was cold. I was shiverin'. Livin' in a cardboard shack'll do 'at to a person. Grady's got blankets.
    CLEMENTINE. Why's he bein' so nice to you? All the pickers hate 'im. He beat ol' Mr. Wittlecarp with a shovel 'cause he couldn't git 'at wooden leg a his to snap inta place fer squattin'. One day, Papa's gonna teach him a thing er two in the fiel'. When he gits his

strength up.

PENNY. Uh huh.

CLEMENTINE. *(Touchin' PENNY'S dress.)* Ya got dirt on yer best dress, on Mama's dress. You been *pickin'* in Mama's dress.

PENNY. Clementine....

CLEMENTINE. You do paint a pi'ture of her in it ... when it's clean.

(PENNY looks down at the dress, painfully. She recovers.)

PENNY. Quit! Quit worryin' 'bout me. *(Beat.)* An' my dress.

CLEMENTINE. You smell like alkee-hol.

PENNY. It's purely medicinal. Dogs bring it to people in the snow. In Switzerlan' er one a them damn foreign countries where winter goes on ever' goddamn day.

CLEMENTINE. Cussin' too?

PENNY. 'Xactly. 'At's why a young lady like misself has the need to hear a few kin' words from a gen'leman ... some goddamn refined conversation!

CLEMENTINE. *(Playfully.)* Grady Gunther, a gen'leman? The man who spits tobaccee like he's tarrin' a rabbit behin' 'im?! *(CLEMENTINE demontrates by play-spittin' frantic'lly behin' her. PENNY is unmoved. CLEMENTINE gives up an' begins to peel a potato. Beat.)* Ya look tired.

PENNY. I needs me a cigarette, 'at's all.

CLEMENTINE. Papa's gonna see you.

PENNY. *(Lights one up.)* Papa ain't seen me in years.

CLEMENTINE. He sees ya.

PENNY. Clementine, cain't nobody see in the dark.

CLEMENTINE. *(Beat. Deflectin'.)* Well ... them shacks need windas! It ain't right. It jus' ain't right.

PENNY. Don't matter none. Seein' ain't knowin'. But then, nobody in this big black worl' knows me, why should he be any dif-f'ernt?

CLEMENTINE. *(Soothin' her.)* Papa loves Penny.

PENNY. Does not.

CLEMENTINE. Papa loves Penny. I knows 'at! He talks 'bout

her all the time.

PENNY. Quit.

CLEMENTINE. Why, he goes on an' on an' on, 'specially when she goes off in strange fiel's. He cries an' misses her somepin awful. Like … like someone dug a well in 'im an' drained the whole ocean out.

PENNY. Who put them lies in yer head?

CLEMENTINE. I got eyes. I got eyes to see me stuff. Stuff 'at ain't so purty!

PENNY. Yer makin' it up. Like ya always do. How the hell would you know anythin' about Papa? He won't even give you the time a day. Never has an' never will, an' 'at's a blessin' in disguise. Amen.

(PENNY crosses herself. CLEMENTINE maintains her optimism.)

CLEMENTINE. Think what you want. But things are changin' aroun' us ever' day. Califor-nee brung it to us! Papa talks to me here.

PENNY. You don't know nothin'.

CLEMENTINE. I knows I has to sing to him, 'til he falls asleep. Poor ol' Papa. He says he ain't got nothin' to live fer, sence he los' Mama…an' now, the lan' done broke his heart.

PENNY. Now I know yer lyin'. Papa ain't got no heart. The liquor drowned it outta his ol' body 'fore you was even born, an' lef' 'im with a sick sperit 'at spits on you an' me—the on'y women that'll give him a second thought.

CLEMENTINE. *(Smilin'.)* He says Mama loved them blue eyes a his. An' I cain't say I blame 'er. It's like he made two little planet earths stan' still, jus' fer you. 'An they's somepin in 'at, Penny.

(PENNY has difficulty with the memory of Mama.)

PENNY. Yeah, Mama. This place woulda got her outta 'at ol' calico bathrobe right quick.

CLEMENTINE. She was always so sick, right? So sick … bless her heart.…

PENNY. All wrapped up sad, starin' at that fiel'.

CLEMENTINE. ...Waitin' to hol' Papa when he come in outta the dirt, I bet.

PENNY. (*Sympathetic to her mother.*) Clementine, she never *could* bring herself to hol' Papa, or his pi'ture when she passed. He may as well poisoned her years before.

CLEMENTINE. A man lost his wife, Penny, jus' the same.

PENNY. Next time he plays 'at violin, jus' give him a bottle of anythin', anythin' resemblin' 'at serpent he guzzles down his wrinkled ol' throat. 'At oughta choke his tears offa ya. Then ya wait. Wait 'til he drinks hisself better. 'At's what Mama did, 'at's what I did, an' now, 'at's what yer gonna do. Give Papa his sweet medicine.

(*PENNY adjus's her little sister's collar. CLEMENTINE looks out inta the fiel' with uncertainty.*)

CLEMENTINE. Fiel's froze up.

PENNY. What?

CLEMENTINE. Heard the boys talkin' while I's still in bed. Looks like them peas was as cold as you was last night, Penny. They might be no good to nobody now. One night of frost ... all them little deaths happenin' while the whole camp lay sleepin'.... It's a shame, ain't it?

PENNY. Ain't no shame. The devil done followed us here. But the sun's comin' up, meltin' 'at cold-blooded night away, an' them peas is gonna be good as gold ... good as gold, jus' like they say.

CLEMENTINE. We's gonna lose days a work 'cause of 'at ruthless ol' ice. The fiel''s gonna starve us again. Starve us all.

(*PENNY grabs her sack an' marches to the edge of the fiel'.*)

PENNY. I said there ain't nothin' wrong with them peas, ya hear?! Yer han's might git a little numb, but you'll git used to it. Now, git yer sack, Clementine.... I don't care if it's snowin', we're pickin' today!

(*CLEMENTINE grabs her sack an' follows, singin', "Hard Times."*

---

*See page three for information on obtaining permission to use this song.

The sisters squat an' pick peas.)

CLEMENTINE. *(Singin'.)*
"Let us pause in life's pleasures an' count its many tears,
 While we all sup sorrow with the poor,

(CLEMENTINE raises her eyebrow to a depressed PENNY, promptin' her to join.)

PENNY and CLEMENTINE. *(Singin'.)*
They's "a song that will linger forever in our ears,
Oh! Hard Times come again no more,

(CLEMENTINE stops singin'. PENNY continues ...)

PENNY. *(Singin'.)*
"Tis the song, the sigh of the weary...."
Hard Times. Hard Times, come again no more. .."

(CLEMENTINE picks each pod with a differ'nt boy's name. It is obvious how she feels about each one ...)

CLEMENTINE. Billy Bob!...
PENNY. *(Singin'.)*
"Many days you have lingered aroun' my cabin door...."
CLEMENTINE. Jimmy Joe....
PENNY. *(Singin'.)*
 "Oh! Hard Times... "
CLEMENTINE. Haskell Lee....
PENNY. *(Singin'.)*
"Come again no more... "
CLEMENTINE. *(Over her singin'.)* ... Lloyd!
PENNY. *(Annoyed; stops singin'.)* Clementine!
CLEMENTINE. Wanna know what I's doin'?
PENNY. I know what yer doin'! Yer doin' what ya always do.
CLEMENTINE. Ask me.
PENNY. Now, why do I have to ask ya, if I already know?

CLEMENTINE. *(Puppy eyes.)* Ask meeeee—

PENNY. Awright! Clementine Ruth ... what'cha do—

CLEMENTINE. I's pickin' boys!

PENNY. Jus' pickin' boys, huh?

CLEMENTINE. 'Stead of jus' pickin' plain ol' peas, I's pickin' boys. Them boys I said.

PENNY. I heard what ya said. *(Beat.)* You been readin' my diary?

CLEMENTINE. No, ma'am.

PENNY. Them boys you said....

CLEMENTINE. I's pickin' all the boys in camp. One by one.

PENNY. Like I said, you been readin' my diary?

CLEMENTINE. *(Teasin' PENNY.)* Oh, no! I's too scairt to ever lay my eyes on such work as 'at! But I have been preparin' misself fer the occasion, should it arise, with Papa's dimestore novels. *(She giggles.)* All those purty words. All 'at moanin' an' groanin' an' flexin' goin' on. I sweat when I jus' think about it. *(Beat.)* I feel pale. Do I look pale?

PENNY. You look pale.

CLEMENTINE. *(Proudly.)* I look pale.

PENNY. Jus' squat, an' pick yer boys. Words to live by.

CLEMENTINE. Words to live by. *(Beat.)* Ya know Penny, peas ain't so bad, when you trick 'em like I do. Givin' 'em a face, a body ... a little hat—

PENNY. Clementine, we are stan'in' on a frozen pea fiel', pickin' pods like ice cubes, fer three cents a box—Ain't no way to make 'at roman'ic!

CLEMENTINE. *(Under her breath.)* Is so.

PENNY. I worry 'bout you.

CLEMENTINE. An' I worry 'bout you!

(Beat. QUINCY'S DOG wanders by, offstage.)

PENNY. Go on! Git! You ol' wiry-hair'd rat-faced belly-fulla-socks!

CLEMENTINE. Ain't it the truth, though!

PENNY. He's gittin' to look more an' more like Quincy ever' day.

CLEMENTINE. Yet somehows, them yella hairs look much better on 'at yummy chunk-of-boy Kransickle, than his dog.

PENNY. Shoo!

CLEMENTINE. All's I know is wherever 'at sack a fleas drags hisself, 'at dream boat of a daddy a his ain't far behin'. *(Primpin'.)* How do I look?

PENNY. Presentable ... fer a dog-faced boy.

CLEMENTINE. *(Proudly.)* I figgered! Some days I don't need much mendin'.

(CLEMENTINE has managed to put a big dirt streak on her face. PENNY motions for her to wipe it off.)

PENNY. Do like 'at.
CLEMENTINE. *(Missin' it.)* Oh … like 'at?
PENNY. No, like 'at.
CLEMENTINE. *(Missin' it.)* Like 'at?
PENNY. Like 'at!
CLEMENTINE. Like 'at?
PENNY. C'mere. You look like a coalminer.
CLEMENTINE. Well, 'at ain't appealin' at all.

(PENNY grabs her face an' spit-cleans it. QUINCY, unseen by audience, is before them in the fiel', offstage. CLEMENTINE looks as if she is meetin' God. She opens her eyes wide an' appears to have stopped breathin'.)

PENNY. Hey Quincy. 'At mutt a yers went over yonder to place 'at runny ol' nose a his under someone else's dress. Hope you got more manners than 'at. *(CLEMENTINE has managed to wipe dirt all over her face again. PENNY covers.)* Oh, uh, we was jus' havin' ourselves a little war paint comp-ee-tition. *(PENNY slaps her on the back.)* You win! *(Still, a frozen CLEMENTINE.)* Clementine....? Don'tcha got nothin' to say to Quincy? *(To QUINCY.)* Well, ya got yerself an eyeful. *(Treatin' him like his dog.)* Go on! Git! Skidaddle!

(Long beat. QUINCY has gone, CLEMENTINE thaws with a jerk.)

CLEMENTINE. *(Weakly.)* Hey, Quincy.

PENNY. He's gone, honey.

CLEMENTINE. *(Weakly.)* Nice mornin', ain't it?

PENNY. Prob'ly went to hunt the garbage fer scraps. Fer hisself, not his dog.

CLEMENTINE. *(Loudly.)* I LIKE YER DOG! I DO!

PENNY. Pipe down er he'll bring his ugly self back here! 'Sides, what do you want with a mulligan like 'at? I'll git ya a big ol' smelly barn cat er somepin. You'd take to that, wouldn' ya?

CLEMENTINE. Oooohh ... that'd be nice.

PENNY. See, yer better off'n me. You got options. Boys ain't ever'thin'.

CLEMENTINE. I do declare, they's Emmet Emerson!

PENNY. WHERE!?

CLEMENTINE. *(Swoonin' over EMMET.)* If boys ain't ever'thin', I'd like me a big ol' plate of nothin' please!

(PENNY spots EMMET EMERSON, who is never seen. He is offstage, in the fiel', a big vision of yummy. PENNY primps subtly.)

PENNY. Yer gonna embarrass us if you don't quit slobberin'.... *(To EMMET.)* Hey Emmet, yer lookin' *big* today. *(Whisperin' to CLEMENTINE.)* Do like 'at. All subtle an' aloft an' mee-sterious like 'at. Yep. 'At's the way to ketch a fish.

(PENNY sways like a ship ready to be docked. CLEMENTINE tries desperately to learn her moves, to no avail.)

CLEMENTINE. *(Whispers to Penny:)* What kinda kitty cat ya gonna git me? Aunt Pat had a cat with spots. Spots jus' like a Guernsey.

PENNY. That Emmet. Um ummmmm ... Nice work if you can git it. *(To EMMET, in her sexiest voice.)* Emmet ... doll ... what'cha pickin' in my fiel' fer?

CLEMENTINE. *(Imitatin' PENNY.)* He's pickin' peas like us, I reckon'. *(Laughs wildly.)* Don't take much of a brainstorm to figure 'at out, silly!

(PENNY shoots her a look, then recovers in her best high class southern accent.)

PENNY. Ya'll will have to excuse my ... my weary baby sista. It appears 'at she has left her wits on the side a the road on our long treacherous journey to Califor-nee.

CLEMENTINE. Lan' o' Plen'y! *(CLEMENTINE looks at PENNY'S mouth.)* Hey Penny, you got somepin in yer teeth—

PENNY. *(Through her teeth.)* PUT A LID ON IT!

CLEMENTINE. *(Pickin' her teeth.)* But Penny—go like 'at ... you got somepin—

PENNY. *(Ignorin' CLEMENTINE.)* SOOOOO ... Emmet, y'all goin' down by the North Forty? 'Coupla boys gittin' together ... playin' a few songs ... havin' a good time, dancin'....?

CLEMENTINE. She's a real good dancer. Like grease on a skillet.

PENNY. *(To EMMET.)* Oh, I'm not 'at good, little one. Git pickin' sista!

CLEMENTINE. *(Defendin' PENNY.)* You is so. SHE IS SO!

PENNY. *(To EMMET.)* Maybe you an' I will find out, darlin'.

CLEMENTINE. *(Copyin' PENNY.)* Darrrrlin'.

PENNY. I'll see ya there, with bells on.

CLEMENTINE. JINGLE JANGLE! *(EMMET is gone. Turnin' to PENNY....)* You got somepin in yer teeth.

PENNY. *(Horrified.)* I do? Was 'at there the whole damn time I was rag-chewin'?

CLEMENTINE. Amen!

PENNY. Why didn't you say somepin?

CLEMENTINE. *(Quotin' PENNY.)* "PUT A LID ON IT!" An' I did ... sista!

PENNY. *(Eyein' the piece of food.)* Dammit all to hell, Emmet probl'y thought I et me a side a beef this mornin'.

CLEMENTINE. Yep. He don't git sausage like we do. We's lucky.

PENNY. *(Beat. Sarcastically.)* Yep, lucky.

(The girls squat an' snap peas again.)

CLEMENTINE. Penny, could I borrow Mama's dress tonight, fer

dancin'? *(PENNY stops at this.)* I'll scrub the dirt outta it. Papa says I should wear more dresses. Papa says.

PENNY. Honey, this dress is fer … well, the growed-up type. It's cut in places you ain't been yet. An' it'll sure as hell make you a woman before yer time. An' you got plen'y of that.

CLEMENTINE. *(Beat.)* Ya miss Jeb?

PENNY. *(Throwin' a pea inta the fiel' with frustration.)* I'm sure he's doin' jus' fine!

CLEMENTINE. But do ya miss 'im?

PENNY. Clementine, if you ever wanna ketch a man, you gotta learn ya the art of speakin' without speakin'… now would be a good time to start practicin'.

CLEMENTINE. *(Namin' the peas as she picks.)* Carl Crowbody … Grady Gunther….
(Punchin' it.) Jeb Tiiii … dwell….

PENNY. I don't wanna talk about it!

(CLEMENTINE picks as she sings, "Hard Times."* PENNY eyes CLEMENTINE regretfully, as if she's kicked a puppy. PENNY digs in her brassiere fer her matches.)

CLEMENTINE. *(Singin'.)*
"Let us pause in life's pleasures an' count our many tears,
While we all sup sorrow with the poor,
There's a song that will linger forever in our ears,
Oh! Hard Times, come again no more."

(A train chugs by. PENNY lights a cigarette. The train passes. PENNY walks deep inta the bleak fiel' as if it has the words to comfort her. She exits. CLEMENTINE follows, wide-eyed. Beat. JEB enters with a suitcase an' rifle.)

JEB. Aloysius, you are slower than a dish of red-eye gravy runnin' up a hill. *(ALOYSIUS enters reluctantly with a knapsack. He holds STUMP, still dead, under his arm. ALOYSIUS surveys the camp, an' manipulates the waggin' of STUMP'S tail. JEB puts his*

---

*See page three for information on obtaining permission to use this song.

belongin's to the side an' looks inta the fiel'.) Sweet Jesus, would ya look at that! Crop as far as the eye can see! Seven cents. They's gonna pay us seven cents a box to pick all 'at green…. Green enough to color the een-tire faded state a Oklahoma.

ALOYSIUS. Califor-nee crop. I don't trust her. Stump don't trust her. Look at 'im. He's actin' funny. Ancy-like an' all. *(STUMP don't move ever, still.)* Mama's gonna whoop ya, quit!

JEB. Aloysius, where's Mama?

ALOYSIUS. *(Beat. Whisperin'.)* In the car.

JEB. We ain't got no car. We hitched.

ALOYSIUS. *(To hisself.)* Mama coulda hitched.

JEB. I'm sorry, I couldn' hear ya … where's Mama?

ALOYSIUS. *(A little louder.)* Away. Mama's gone away. On a long trip.

JEB. 'At's right. An' to where?

ALOYSIUS. *(Painfully.)* To h-h-h-heav'n.

JEB. 'At's right again. An' what else can ya tell me?

ALOYSIUS. She's jus' visitin' 'til we gits there.

(ALOYSIUS looks to heaven an' waves.)

JEB. Yep.

ALOYSIUS. Yep. *(Testin' JEB.)* But thank the Lord, Sweet Jesus … I still got Stump.

JEB. (*Bitin' his lip.*) Yep, ya still got Stump, little brother.

ALOYSIUS. Perky as ever!

JEB. Yep.

ALOYSIUS. An' did ya see how he et up his breakfast? Another bite outta 'at corncob. Still got his puppy app-ee-tite!

JEB. Yep.

(ALOYSIUS sets STUMP down, an' places a half-eaten corncob in his mouth.)

ALOYSIUS. Stump sit! Lay down. Now … WHEN YOU SPOTS PENNY AND CLEMENTINE, GIVE US A GOOD CLEAN BARK. SOMEPIN SIMPLE-LIKE SO AS NOT TO ALERT THE WOMEN-

FOLK!

JEB. Quit yer bellerin' an' git yer ducks in a row!

ALOYSIUS. Think the girls'll be happy to see us?

JEB. 'At's a silly question. Course they'll be happy to see us. *(Beat.)* Why wouldn' they be happy to see us?

ALOYSIUS. *(Shrugs.)* Maybe they don' like us no more.

JEB. They don' gotta like us. Penny an' me is gittin' married, an' at makes us "kin." An' 'at word erases them kinda concerns. Like when Mama use' ta burn a biscuit now an' then … nobody said nothin', we jus' ate aroun' it. It's a rule, a way of livin'. Now' I made you a promise, I'm gonna gitcha fam'ly again...

ALOYSIUS. *(Stuck on MAMA.)* Mama don't burn biscuits. Mama's biscuits is like … like angels' bread. Like 'at.

JEB. Aloysius … we needs these women! Now they's gonna like us if I has to spit sugar on 'em ever' damn day! At's love! Good lovin'! *(Beat. Arrogantly.)* 'Sides, we got fine breedin', we're good lookin', an' we're as normal as the next fella. What's not to like?

ALOYSIUS. Think Mama's hungry? It's about supper time.

JEB. *(Beat, Givin' up.)* Hey … Ysius … how about a good game of hide n' seek?

(ALOYSIUS tags JEB, knockin' him down.)

ALOYSIUS. YER IT! *(He runs a couple of feet.)* COUNT TO TEN!

(ALOYSIUS runs offstage.)

JEB. One, two—
ALOYSIUS. *(Runnin' back on, threat'nin'.)* SLOWER!
JEB. *(Beat)* Oooooonnnnneeeee … Twwwwoooooooooo ....

(As JEB counts, he sneaks over to STUMP, takes a bite outta the corncob, spits it to the side, an' places it back in STUMP'S jaws. JEB exits to look fer ALOYSIUS. DUSTY enters, sits on an ol' fruit crate, an' plays a seductive instrumen'al tune. PENNY comes out of the Bumpinmeyer shack in a dress that could make

the peas thaw. She begins to dance to the Devil's banjo.
CLEMENTINE comes outta the shack, dressed in a fluffy pink, girlish
dress, an' bows in her hair. She smiles at the sight of PENNY
dancin'. DUSTY stops, tips his hat, an' gits. PENNY stops dan-
cin' an' calls after him.)

PENNY. Hey mister ... don' stop! Don' stop yer music. I'll jus'
die if you do.

CLEMENTINE. *(To DUSTY.)* Play somepin fer lovers. *(Beat.*
Angrily.) PLAY MISTER!

(PENNY turns to fin' CLEMENTINE wrapped aroun' herself like a
daddy long-legs in a whirlwin'.)

PENNY. Clementine ... yer in a mood. An' yer all gussied up,
like a ... like a ... right proud piece of cotton candy er somepin.

CLEMENTINE. *(Flattered.)* Ohhhhh, this ol' dog-eared dress?
(Beat.) Yer dancin' again.

PENNY. Yep. Fer the first time, my feet quit strugglin' with this
godfersaken groun', jus' long enough fer it to trick me, an' make sure
I's still drawn to it. *(Kneelin', she speaks to the dirt.)* I'll still dance
on ya, jus' like you will, over my grave.

(CLEMENTINE sees STUMP, who never ever moves, ever.)

CLEMENTINE. Well, I'll be a reindeer in the summertime! Ain't
'at Stump layin' there eatin' up 'at corncob ... toyin' with 'at corncob
... lookin' at that corncob?

PENNY. *(Worried.)* Jeb! Jeb Tidwell ... in Califor-nee.

CLEMENTINE. Ain't 'at the most roman'ic thing you ever did
hear? *(Pulls out her harmonica an' gives a dramatic toot....)* A
MAN ...led by his true love fer a woman, crossin' many states an'
overcomin' perilous odds in the face a death, to see her again!
(Another dramatic chord.) AN' NOW ... his trusty canine, hot on the
trail of the fersaken one, can fin'lly rest as he signals to his master 'at
the search has ended! *(She hyperventilates as if her lungs cain't take*
much more drama.) I feel pale. *(Beat.)* I FEEL PALE, PENNY!

PENNY. I feel pale, too.
CLEMENTINE. You look pale.
PENNY. Jeb's come all this way.

(CLEMENTINE sees an offstage QUINCY.)

CLEMENTINE. Howdy Quincy! Yer lookin' ... cleaner 'an usual.... *(Beat.)* Ohhhh, well, do ya like cotton candy? *(Beat.)* Dance? Together, ya mean? *(Beat.)* Okey dokey. Come an' git me ... ON A SLOW ONE. I'll be here. *(Rushes to PENNY in a panic.)* Penny, ya gotta learn me some of them dancin' hijinxes of yers. Quick, 'fore he loses int'rest in the whole idea!
PENNY. *(Still in shock.)* What in God's name am I gonna do?

(CLEMENTINE poses with her arms outstretched an' tries to lure PENNY to dance with a seductive tone ...)

CLEMENTINE. C'mon Penny ... I'll count.
PENNY. Awright. Awright!

(They begin to dance, but PENNY is preoccupied.)

CLEMENTINE. One two three ... one two three ... I's dancin'! Boy is Aloysius gonna be suprised! One two—Aloysius has got eyes like Papa ...'cept they's brown ... an' smaller, an' a diff'ernt shape ... but they's somepin in 'at, Penny!
PENNY. *(Suddenly pullin' away.)* Clementine! I ... I cain't dance right now!

(STUMP barks. The girls look at the dead dog in bewilderment.)

PENNY and CLEMENTINE. Nah.

(Beat. ALOYSIUS flies in like a bat outta hell. He don't see the girls, as he interrogates STUMP.)

ALOYSIUS. What's all the hub-bub? THINK BOY, THINK!...

Hmm ... if I was a dog, how would I talk to me?

PENNY and CLEMENTINE. *(From behin' him.)* ALOYSIUS!!

ALOYSIUS. *(Jumpin' outta his skin.)* AAAAAAHHHHH! *(Holdin' his heart.)* Penny! Clementine! You shouldn' sneak up on a fella like 'at! Well ... how y'all gittin' on? Ya'll don' look no older er fatter er nothin'.

CLEMENTINE. You still got enough charm to choke a horse, Aloysius.

PENNY. Where's 'at bullheaded brother a yers?

(JEB backs on-stage, his shirt torn an' his han' over one eye. He appears to have been rumblin'. He yells to the men offstage. The men are never seen.)

JEB. Y'ALL SAY THAT AGAIN AN' THEY'S GONNA BE HELL TO PAY! YA HEAR ME! DAMN FOOLS! *(JEB an' PENNY see each other an' the worl' stops. Beat.)* Hey Penny.

PENNY. Hey cowboy.

JEB. Hey Penny.

PENNY. Hey Cowboy.

JEB. *(Drawin' attention to his eye.)* Owie.

PENNY. What happened?

JEB. Got hit.

PENNY. Who did 'at to ya'?

(PENNY an' JEB circle each other in a sort of matin' dance. JEB performs his version of foreplay.)

JEB. Well, I was jus' askin' yer whereabouts, when some lunkhead starts mouthin' off about how he put the blocks to ya. So, I went inta the fiel' to calm down, an' did what I always do to ree-lax... I dismantled me an ol' wheel plough mouldboard with connectin' hake chain an' adjus'able yoke, got me a more stubborn-than-the-day-is-long horse outta the corral to he'p me drag it on back, an' when I knocked him out cold with one glorious swoop, then his buddy punched me! Is 'at fella rude, er what?

(PENNY an' JEB kiss hungrily.)

    CLEMENTINE. *(Remindin' her.)* "Perilous odds!" Penny.
    PENNY. *(Breakin' away.)* Was this fellar's name Billy Bob?
    JEB. Nope.
    PENNY. Tommy Ray?
    JEB. Nope.
    PENNY. Haskell Lee?
    JEB. Nope.
    PENNY. Lloyd?

(JEB hunches over in his usual "belly cramp" routine due to the
    subject of PENNY'S conquests.)

    JEB. Don' know why, but I feel sick in my belly. I got a bad
feelin'.
    ALOYSIUS. Maybe it's cuz Penny's been scratchin' every itch in
camp.
    JEB. *(Defensively.)* What did you say little brother?!
    PENNY. *(Distractin' him.)* Babydoll! Dance with me. Dance
with me.

(PENNY gives JEB that "look," an' he is mesmerized again. They
    begin to slow dance. JEB is in heaven as PENNY closes her eyes
    with guilt an' emotion. CLEMENTINE an' ALOYSIUS watch the
    two lovebirds.)

    CLEMENTINE. T'ain't nothin' wrong with 'at pi'ture
right'chere. Jus' like peanut butter an' jelly, 'at's what they is.

(ALOYSIUS eyes CLEMENTINE'S dress an' sees the cotton candy
    resemblance.)

    ALOYSIUS. You look like you should jump on a stick with 'at
dress on.
    CLEMENTINE. Why, thankee!

(JEB an' PENNY slink to the groun' awkwardly, as they kiss an' grope. ALOYSIUS an' CLEMENTINE ignore them as if it is as normal as watchin' the crop grow, liftin' their voices to climb over the moanin' an' groanin' an' flexin' goin' on.)

PENNY. Jeb darlin'....
JEB. I missed you, sweet pea....
PENNY. I know ya did....
JEB. Ya miss me?
PENNY. *(Kisses him.)* Well ... sure....
CLEMENTINE. Whatcha doin' Aloysius?
ALOYSIUS. This minute?
CLEMENTINE. Uh huh.
ALOYSIUS. Nothin'.
CLEMENTINE. *(Squeals.)* You ain't lost a way with a phrase!

(PENNY an' JEB continue to ravage one another....)

PENNY. What, doll?
JEB. I said, did ya miss me?
PENNY. *(Somepin pokes her.)* Ow!

(JEB takes a shiny object outta his pocket an' tosses it nonchalantly.)

JEB. Sorry, straight edge razor—
PENNY. 'At's why yer so smooth....

(CLEMENTINE an' ALOYSIUS raise their voices a bit.)

CLEMENTINE. Yer all growed-up into yer man shape!
ALOYSIUS. So is you!
CLEMENTINE. Aloysius, ya catch more flies with sugar than salt.
ALOYSIUS. I knows 'at.
CLEMENTINE. Then sweeten them han's up so's I can stick to 'em.

(PENNY an' JEB have a few less items of clothin' on.)

JEB. You piece a heav'n you....
PENNY. Ohhh say it like it is ... Ow!

(JEB pulls another shiny object from his pocket.)

JEB. Fork. Mama's silver.
PENNY. I don't care.
JEB. *(Drops it.)* Yes ma'am.

(Intertwined, JEB an' PENNY begin to crawl offstage. JEB pulls a few more pieces of silverware from his pockets an' throws 'em to the side. CLEMENTINE an' ALOYSIUS struggle to be heard.)

CLEMENTINE. LOOK INTO MY EYES, ALOYSIUS ... WHAT DO YOU SEE?
ALOYSIUS. REE-FLECTION. REE-FLECTION OF ME.
CLEMENTINE. 'AT'S RIGHT ... YOUUUUUU.
JEB. Barn?
PENNY. *(Kissin' him.)* Ain't no barn....
JEB. I'll fin' one....
PENNY. *(Another kiss.)* ...Fer miles....
JEB. I'll build one!

(PENNY an' JEB crawl offstage. ALOYSIUS moves like a monkey in front of a mirror, catchin' his reflection in CLEMENTINE'S eyes, 'til he realizes that they are alone. CLEMENTINE moves in fer the kill.)

CLEMENTINE. Mr. Tidwell ... you do somepin to me ... somepin 'at jus' ain't fit fer public viewin'. Now, ya don' have to court me. We can skip right to the good part—cut through the crust an' git to the custard!
ALOYSIUS. You Califor-nee girls sure are on a schedule. Back home, we'd jus' be gittin' to horseshoes, er shootin' the can off the fence about now.

CLEMENTINE. Aloysius, I don't ask fer much, but THE CROP IS WINKIN' AN' I'S READY TO BE LIFTED UP! RIGHT'CHERE. … Aloysius, kiss me. I wanna see my angel.

(CLEMENTINE grabs him an' kisses him, wrestlin' him to the groun'. After a struggle, ALOYSIUS ketches his breath. CLEMENTINE stan's, looks anxiously out to the fiel', arms lifted up, waitin' fer the angel to carry her away.)

ALOYSIUS. Clementine, yer a nice girl, but you make me tired.
CLEMENTINE. *(Closin' her eyes, still waitin'.)* SSSHHHH!
ALOYSIUS. *(Gigglin'.)* Ain't no one comin' fer you. Ain't no one comin' fer a little girl.

(CLEMENTINE opens her eyes an' turns to him, incensed.)

CLEMENTINE. I AIN'T NO GIRL! I … am a woman! A modern woman with needs an' stuff! Aloysius, if you don't want me, why don't ya jus' say so!
ALOYSIUS. *(Under his breath.)* So.
CLEMENTINE. Speak up. Be a man fer once!
ALOYSIUS. SO! SO SO SO!
CLEMENTINE. *(Beat; crushed.)* Oh. Well … 'at's jus' fine. *(Beat. She looks to GRADY'S shack.)* I got me a boyfrien' anyways. I's jus' tryin' to hol' on to a slice a home, I reckon. Ya know, Aloysius, I been sayin' "Good-bye" sence the day I was born. I let my Mama go…. God took 'er. I let our lan' go…. Dust took 'im. An' now, I 'spose it's time…. Time I let you go…. It's my trouble, come again. *(She walks to GRADY'S shack an' turns.)* We coulda all been saved. Now, 'at's a shame, ain't it?

(CLEMENTINE goes inta GRADY'S shack, upset, leavin' ALOYSIUS speechless. Beat.)

ALOYSIUS. Clementine? *(He draws in the dirt.)* Drew you a flower!… *(ALOYSIUS stan's outside GUNTHER'S shack an' sings softly:)*

"Oh my darlin', Oh my darlin', Oh my darlin' Clementine....
Oh my darlin', Oh my darlin'.....

*(ALOYSIUS holds STUMP close as he hears CLEMENTINE inside,
gigglin'. He covers his ears to block the sound. Lights fade as the
dark creeps in. ALOYSIUS rocks hisself to sleep. Lights fade up
as early mornin' approaches.*
PENNY an' JEB enter in a tiff, puttin' on they's clothes.)

PENNY. You ain't changed one iota, Jeb Tidwell!

JEB. Ain't you the pot callin' the kettle black! Apparen'ly, the
state a Oklahoma t'weren't big enough fer you to dance on!

PENNY. Yer jus' tryin' to control me like some dumb animal in
a tornada, an' I got news fer you, mister.... I's doin' jus' fine by myself.

JEB. By yerself? How would you know? You ain't never been by
yerself! If you didn' have a man aroun' to make sure yer purty, you'd
disappear like a shadow 'at passes over a fiel'.

PENNY. Why don't you jus' pack up yer silver, yer pie in the
sky, an' go on back to 'at ghost town, 'cause Clementine an' I don'
need yer he'p! *(Beat. To ALOYSIUS.)* Where is Clementine?
(ALOYSIUS shrugs.) She sleepin'? Aloysius?!

(PENNY grabs ALOYSIUS, but JEB steps in.)

JEB. You don' need our he'p, 'member?

*(PENNY glares at a guilty ALOYSIUS, tryin' to intimidate him to
crack. JEB glares at PENNY. JEB gives ALOYSIUS a "look,"
tellin' him to keep quiet. ALOYSIUS pets STUMP. PENNY goes
to set down, lights one up, as the sun rises. Long fade up.*
*An hour has passed. PENNY'S cigarette is out. CLEMENTINE,
looped, giggles an' exits GRADY'S shack, stoppin' when she sees
the three starin' at her. PENNY rises like a feather on a rooster
at a cockfight.)*

PENNY. What're you doin'? *(Beat.)* You better dig down an' fin'

some words to come out 'fore I make up my own answer. *(Beat.)*
Clementine? What was ya doin' in there?!

CLEMENTINE. Nothin'.

PENNY. Nothin'?! *(Beat.)* Yer blin' drunk!

CLEMENTINE. It's purely medicinal.

PENNY. Don't git smart with me, young lady.

CLEMENTINE. We should git pickin'.

PENNY. Sun jus' come up. Sides, ya look like hell.

CLEMENTINE. I needs me a cigarette, at's all.

PENNY. Now, here's where yer real careful, darlin', 'cause from
the looks a this, I'm buildin' a fire 'nough to burn this whole camp
down. Now I'm gonna ask you one more time, what are you doin'
stumblin' outta Grady Gunther's shack at five o'clock in the mornin'?

CLEMENTINE. *(Defiantly.)* I was cold. I was cold like you was
cold, so instead a stealin' another blanket, I went in where it was
warm. Where I could smother myself in down, an' liquor, an' some
goddamn re-fined conversation, sister! *(CLEMENTINE pulls a sausage from under her garter, an' slaps it in PENNY'S han'.)* Cook it
up!

PENNY. I'm gonna kill him!

(PENNY goes toward GRADY'S shack. CLEMENTINE stops her.)

CLEMENTINE. Penny don't! You'll embarrass me! *(Beat.)*
Please...?!

(PENNY sees the boys listenin'. She lowers her voice. Beat.)

PENNY. Clementine, you gotta lot to learn about this rotten ol'
life. He took somepin from you, somepin you cain't ever git back, an'
then paid fer it with the cheap meat he throws outside fer the dogs!

CLEMENTINE. You do it!

PENNY. *(Beat.)* 'At's diff'ernt!

JEB. *(To PENNY.)* You do it? Penny? What's she talkin' about?

PENNY. She's jus' upset. Somepin on'y kin would know.

ALOYSIUS. *(Whisperin' in a panic.)* Jeb? They don like us no
more! We come all this way fer nothin'. Nothin'!

PENNY. *(Manipulatively.)* She needs herself a big black cup a coffee, 'at's all. *(Beat.)* Well, are you jus' gonna stan' there er are you gonna fetch it?!

(PENNY walks to JEB an' kisses him hard. JEB backs away, as he sees what PENNY has become for the first time. ALOYSIUS, panicked, tries to keep in good with PENNY.)

ALOYSIUS. I'll fetch it! I'll fetch it! Yes ma'am!

(As ALOYSIUS dutifully goes to the fire an' pours a cup of coffee, JEB sits with his head in his han's. PENNY pulls CLEMENTINE to the side, so the boys cain't hear.)

PENNY. Now you listen here, not that it's any a yer business, but I already got my somepin taken from me a long time ago, t'weren't nothin' lef' fer Grady.

CLEMENTINE. Givin' it, takin' it, don't matter now, it's gone!

PENNY. *(Beat; touchin' CLEMENTINE'S cheek softly.)* 'At man don' make the cold go away. 'At man is the cold! His han's ain't healin', his words ain't the truth, an' his lovin' ain't no lovin' at all!

CLEMENTINE. *(Loudly, backin' away.)* How would you know what lovin' is! Yer jus' jealous! YOU WANT HIM TO YERSELF! PAPA TOL' ME!

PENNY. Papa tol' you? Papa tol' you nothin'!

(The boys hear this.)

CLEMENTINE. Papa tol' me what you do to Grady, to ev'ry man ... trick 'em, give yer body to 'em, talk nice to 'em ... fer money, fer sausage, sometimes jus' fer nickles to put in the jukebox so's you can dance.

PENNY. Is 'at right? Did Papa happen to mention how we's eatin' on three cents a bucket?

ALOYSIUS. Seven. Posters say seven cents.

PENNY. *(To JEB an' ALOYSIUS.)* Three. Cain't even feed your dead dog on 'at.

(ALOYSIUS looks down at STUMP an' deals with this horrible news.)

CLEMENTINE. Papa says 'at price suits ya. So's you can sell yerself like a box a fruit an' call it "hardship." Papa says its gotten so bad, you cain't even love fer free no more!

(PENNY says nothin', which says it all.)

JEB. Well, ain't ya gonna say somepin? Penny? *(Beat.)* I never thought I'd see the day, my Penny on her back in a barn fer some spare change.

PENNY. This is 'bout fam'ly. It ain't yer place.

ALOYSIUS. *(Panicked.)* Jeb?! Talk to her. Peanut butter an' jelly! Peanut butter an' je—

JEB. You sleepin' with me fer my silver? *(Emptyin' his pockets.)* Fer razors an' forks...? Or did I jus' git lucky, one of yer "charitable poor?"

PENNY. Yep, lucky!

JEB. 'At's a sad, sad story. Guess 'at makes me a fool. What's worse, if yer papa's right, guess 'at makes you a whore.

PENNY. *(Beat.)* A whore? *(Ironically, she laughs.)* Well, Papa oughta know … he made me inta one.

(A long beat.)

CLEMENTINE. Penny—

PENNY. He took my somepin from me an' I will never be warm again.

(Beat. JEB, ALOYSIUS, an' CLEMENTINE look as if they have seen a ghost.)

JEB. Good Lord in heaven.

CLEMENTINE. *(Softly, convincin' herself.)* Yer lyin'. She's lyin'!

ALOYSIUS. Yer Papa cain't do that. 'At's a sin!

(JEB tries to comfort PENNY. PENNY walks toward the fiel' in a daze. Her han's shake as she tries to fin' the matches in her brassiere ... the cigarette falls from her mouth, as a hopelessness overtakes her.)

CLEMENTINE. My papa's a God-fearin' man.

PENNY. Clementine, you don' know Papa. He ain't no saint, an' he sure as hell don' walk on water!

CLEMENTINE. I don' know why yer sayin' all this. I think 'at's horrible. I think yer horrible!

JEB. 'At's yer sister. Have some respect!

PENNY. You got eyes to see ya stuff! Stuff 'at ain't so purty. So tell me, Clementine, yer angel lift you up in there? *(Pointin' to GRADY'S shack.)*

ALOYSIUS. Did yer papa hurt ya?

PENNY. Er were you jus' too dirty? Filthy dirty, jus' like me.

CLEMENTINE. Papa loves Penny. Papa loves Penny.

ALOYSIUS. He ain't yer Papa no more! Not if I has anythin' to say about it!

CLEMENTINE. Papa loves Penny!

JEB. Quiet! Ain't you done enough, Clementine!

CLEMENTINE. Papa's a good man!

JEB. *(Gittin' his rifle.)* We'll see about that!

ALOYSIUS. He's a monster!

JEB. 'At bastard ain't never gonna bother y'all again!

CLEMENTINE. *(Grabbin' the rifle.)* Don't you hurt my papa!

JEB. Dammit, Clementine—!!

(Beat. An awkward silence. CLEMENTINE points the gun at PENNY, an' slowly walks toward her.)

CLEMENTINE. Yer tryin' to tear this fam'ly apart! I hate you. I hate you fer temptin' Papa ... seducin' him, seducin' him with them ways a yers. Layin' yerself down fer anythin' to stick in ya! Ya prob'ly asked fer it!

(PENNY slaps CLEMENTINE, knockin' her to the floor.)

JEB. Penny!

(Long beat. CLEMENTINE, in shock, slowly gits to her knees ... then softly, in her own worl' ...)

CLEMENTINE. We use' ta sing in church ever' Sund'y. Kneelin' an' singin'…. Me, Papa, Mama an'... Me, Papa, Mama an'... Me, Papa, Mama an'—

PENNY. Say it! Say it! Where was I? Where was the "faithless child"... the one who weren't allowed on 'at holy groun', on accounta her illness? Little Penelope, at home under the covers where the sickness began, nursin' her soreness leftover from Papa's Saturd'y night. Do you know what Papa was prayin' fer, while you an' Mama was singin' in the choir? He was prayin' his little girl 'at he ripped the night before, would stay quietly in bed, 'stead a runnin' in an' spillin' his secret all over the congregation.

CLEMENTINE. You coulda run to the fiel'. Fiel' woulda saved ya.

PENNY. I went to yer fiel' in the rain an' the dark. It wouldn' hide me with it's thinnin' crop. Papa circled an' cackled in his unbuttoned trousers…. What's 'at he use' ta say, what's 'at?… *(As PAPA.)* "I LOST ONE LITTLE GIRL IN THE FIEL', BUT THEY'S ANOTHER IN THE HOUSE!" 'At ol' fiel' spit me out, like it was keepin' the peace. I cursed it an' swore it had sacrificed me. But 'at's when I knew ... if Papa couldn' have me, he'd a come after you.

CLEMENTINE. *(Turnin' away an' hidin' her face.)* Don't tell me no more! Don't tell me no more!

PENNY. Look at me! I lived with Mama's back to me while she was alive, payin' fer somepin I didn' ask fer. Mama knew. Mama knew an' took it to her grave, but I ain't takin' it to mine! She lef' me in that dirty ol' house with him when she died, when she died from the sight a you ... another little girl to keep her husband deep in unspeakable truth. An' God forgive me fer sayin' this, but nobody was smilin' when you was born, on that dark dark day, 'cept Papa, mad with plannin', over yer cradle. So if you an' yer mighty fiel' see somepin' you don't like, you an' Mama are the reasons why. An' if I'm a whore the rest of my life ... it's yer fault. It's yer fault! It's somebody's goddamn fault!

JEB. Penny ... think about what yer sayin'.

PENNY. I'm sayin' I gave myself to Papa. I'm sayin' it! Fifteen years he had me in that black bedroom ... the sacrifice, fer Clementine. Fer baby Clementine Ruth.

(PENNY drops to the ground. CLEMENTINE faces the fiel', devastated. Long beat.)

CLEMENTINE. *(Weakly.)* I feel pale. I feel pale, Penny.

JEB. We'll fix this, darlin'. We'll fix this all up.

PENNY. Yer own blood floppin' on ya since you was old enough to walk, sweatin' an' gruntin' an' leavin' his face on ever' man 'at'll ever touch you the rest of yer pathetic life. Think you can fix 'at? *(Beat.)* Yer jus' like the lan 'at looks up my dress, an' spits at me when I ask fer respect. You ain't no diff'ernt.

CLEMENTINE. *(Quotin' PENNY, she realizes that she is to blame.)* "It's somebody's goddamn fault. It's somebody's goddamn fault."

(CLEMENTINE begins her long walk toward the fiel'.)

ALOYSIUS. Yer a nice girl, Clementine....

JEB. We'll fix this all up.

(PENNY pushes her fingers through the earth. She holds her dirty han's up.)

PENNY. It's time you see me fer what I am! I'm dirty. I'm dirty an' I ain't never gonna come clean.

JEB. Yer still the purtiest girl a man ever did see.

ALOYSIUS. *(To CLEMENTINE.)* Drew you a flower. In the dust, Clementine.

CLEMENTINE. Seems ever'thin' I touch turns to dust. An' they's somepin in 'at. They's somepin in 'at, Penny!

JEB. Penny! Penny...

PENNY. I ain't never gonna come clean. Never gonna come

clean.

    ALOYSIUS. They's a song named "Clementine." Clementine?
    CLEMENTINE. Sacrifice...
    PENNY. Sweet undyin' sacrifice.

(Lullin' herself, CLEMENTINE walks with the rifle toward the fiel', singin' "Leavin' Blues."*)

    CLEMENTINE. *(Singin'.)*
They's ... "grasshoppers in my pillow, baby...."
    ALOYSIUS. Clementine...!
    JEB. Penny! Penny!
    CLEMENTINE. *(Singin'.)*
"Crickets all in my meal...."
    PENNY. We ain't never gonna git outta this black fiel'! Do you
hear me?
    ALOYSIUS. *(Callin' to heaven fer help.)* Mama? Mama?
    PENNY. We ain't never gonna git outta this black fiel'.
    CLEMENTINE. *(Singin'.)*
They's ... "grasshoppers in my pillow, Mama...."
    PENNY. *(Hollerin' to CLEMENTINE.)* Stop that goddamn
singin'!

(Silence. The stage goes black 'cept fer a beam of light on CLEMENTINE.)

    CLEMENTINE. It's my trouble, come again.

(CLEMENTINE stan's in the fiel', cocks the rifle, puts the butt of the gun in the dirt an' the tip in her mouth. Blackout. Gunshot.)

---

*See page three for information on obtaining permission to use this song.

SCENE 3

(A black fiel'. DUSTY sits on a fruit crate, plunkin' "Leavin' Blues."*
The lights lift as if the sun is risin'.
ALOYSIUS, JEB, an' PENNY form a tableau of diff'ernt fiel' poses--
ALOYSIUS kneels, JEB stands holdin' a kerchief to his mouth,
an' PENNY sits pushin' her fingers in the dirt. CLEMENTINE
remains lifeless on stage.)

ALOYSIUS. Sun's up. Mama's smilin'. Stump's sleepin'. An' Clementine's singin'. I's an onion picker. Is what I am. Is what I was, when my throat found itself fightin' with a piece a crop I grew mis-self. *(Layin' down.)* I layed down in the dirt, chokin' on the gold of the earth. I went quietly as I drew my last breath, an' let the lan' roll over me.

(ALOYSIUS curls up on the groun' an' shuts his eyes.)

JEB. 'At godforsaken smell stained my fingers as I clenched my heart an' fell to my fate. *(He clutches his arm an' gently falls to his knees.)* I died alone, cryin' fer someone to hear me. *(JEB shuts his eyes.)*

PENNY. I looked out inta the fiel' an' realized ... I'm nothin'. My han's wrinkled in the sun, my curves lost their shape, an' my feet stuck to the groun'. I died an' ol' woman, sufferin' from the same illness I had as a child...blackness. An' there the devil sat, in his shack, laughin', ferver an' ever.

(PENNY pushes her han's inta the dirt an' looks inta the fiel'.
DUSTY stops playin' an' laughs quietly. The lights fade.)

---

*See page three for information on obtaining permission to use this song.

COSTUME PLOT

ACT I

DUSTY
Faded checked shirt
Faded blue jeans
Brown work boots
Brown hat
Faded red kerchief

JEB TIDWELL
Faded blue-jean workpants
Faded blue kerchief in pocket
Faded yellow work shirt
Brown suspenders
Faded red cap with holes
Yellow work boots

ALOYSIUS TIDWELL
Faded blue-jean overalls
Faded orange work shirt
Straw hat with holes
Brown work boots

PENNY BUMPINMEYER
Floral dress, spotted with
    dirt
Black heels

CLEMENTINE BUMPINMEYER
Faded blue-jean overalls
Faded pink blouse
Brown work shoes

ACT II Scene 1

DUSTY
Same as Act I

JEB TIDWELL
Faded brown workpants
Faded red work shirt
Same brown suspenders
Same faded red cap
Same yellow work boots
Blue Jacket

ALOYSIUS TIDWELL
Faded blue workpants
Faded blue work shirt
Same brown work boots
Same straw hat
Red plaid jacket

PENNY BUMINMEYER
Floral dress
Same black heels
Nylons with runs and garter

CLEMENTINE BUMPINMEYER
Bluejeans
Faded yellow blouse
Same brown work shoes

COSTUME PLOT

ACT II Scene 2

PENNY BUMPINMEYER
Same floral dress
Same black heels
Same nylons with runs and garter
Blue sweater
Cut sweater arms used as
    leggings/nylons

CLEMENTINE BUMPINMEYER
Same blue jeans
Same faded yellow blouse
Same brown work shoes
Yellow sweater
Cut sweater arms used as
    leggings/nylons

ACT II Scene 3

JEB TIDWELL
Same as Scene 1
Add blue jacket

ALOYSIUS TIDWELL
Same as Scene 1
Add yellow jacket

PENNY BUMPINMEYER
Blue party dress
Same nylons with runs and garter
Same black heels

CLEMENTINE BUMPINMEYER
Pink party dress
Nylons with runs and garter
Black shoes

PROPERTY PLOT

ACT I

Dirt (Set according to Ground
    Plan)
Dried out onion Down Center
Two dried weeds Down Center
Milk can used as slop bucket Up-
    stage Right of Porch
Pitchfork Left of Door
Scythe Right of Door
Horseshoe hanging crooked over
    door
Petrified dead dog (Yellow Lab)
    Down Left
Clothesline in between tree and
    porch
Clothespins on clothesline
Mama's big floral dress hanging
    on clothesline
Mama's big brassiere hanging on
    clothesline
Mama's big nylon stockings hang-
    ing on clothesline
Tumbleweed Right of Porch

ACT II

Scene One
Dirt (Set according to Ground
    Plan)
Washboard and lantern in front
    of Up Right shack
Two pea-picking sacks and two
    fruit crates in front of Up
    Left shack
Barrel with water Down Right of
    Center
Fruit crate Down Right of Center
Wood stool Up Left
Wood stool Up Right
Clothesline strung between two
    shacks
Clothespins
Papa's trousers
Papa's longjohns
Papa's socks

Scene Two
Add:
Fire pit Down Left with:
    Firewood (half-burnt)
    Fire grill
    Skillet
    Coffee pot
    Coffee mug
    One sausage in skillet

HAND PROPS

ACT I

Faded red kerchief full of dust
(Jeb)
Butterscotch unwrapped (Jeb)
Mouth harp (Jeb)
Two spoons (Aloysius)

ACT II

Scene 1
Suitcase (Jeb)
Three onions (Jeb, Aloysius,
Clementine)

Scene 2
Harmonica (Clementine)
Two sausages (Penny)
Knife and potato (Clementine)
Hairpins (Penny)
Rolled cigarette (Penny)
Matches (Penny)
Two picking sacks (Clementine,
Penny)
Two pairs of gloves with fingers
cut out (Penny, Clementine)

Scene 3
Hunting rifle (Jeb)
Suitcase (Jeb)
Petrified dead dog (Yellow Lab)
(Aloysius)
Dried corncob with a bite out of it
(Aloysius)
Bottle of bourbon (Clementine)
Rolled cigarette (Penny)
Matches (Penny)

CHARACTER NOTES

ALOYSIUS: He isn't retarded. He isn't stupid. He is simply in love
with his farm, his brother, his mother, and his dog. He resists being a
man, due to the horrible circumstances that he would have to face if
he grew up. He can busy himself in creative ways, emphasizing the
most important aspect of Aloysius, his true childlike spirit. He lives in
his own world, but surprises everyone with his profound awareness of
the crop and it's needs. He is a good-hearted, optimist, with a dark
reality to face. Aloysius is the sweet purity of us all and the essence of
the innocence we try to hold onto.

JEB: He is my Everyman. Stay away from a one-noted angry bully
interpretation. Jeb has a good reason for his impatience, his temper
tantrums, his need to be a man, his need for female attention. His
mother ignored him, his father beat him, and his brother is a true lost
little lamb. Without these circumstances, Jeb would lead a very differ-
ent life. But, in the wake of losing his family, his farm, his girlfriend,
and his hope, he does his best to keep the family together. He does
have a temper, he does have yelling fits, he does have an old fash-
ioned idea of women--but he also has heart. Jeb can miraculously pull
the audience into his sadness at the end of Act One. The "Death of
Mama," speech can be the heart of his bitter onion...It can turn his
arrogant harsh character into a delicious vulnerable child. Revel in
this unexpected flip.

CLEMENTINE: The mirror image of Aloysius. She is another childlike dreamer. She loves the crop, her sister, Aloysius, and her papa
more than a look into her own mirror. She can be more fun than a
puppy chasing bubbles; but, the biggest challenge of this freckle-faced
girl, is to plant the seeds of her instability in the first act with a subtle
shovel. Remember she idolizes her sister, and this fact crushes the
audience when her sister blames her for her troubled life at the end.
With Clementine, you will find that you reap what you sew. Give her
a ladder of optimism to climb, but show the cracks in the rungs and it
will save you. She is not unlike Aloysius, a delicate egg that breaks all
our hearts when she is suddenly dropped to her emotional death.

PENNY: The mirror image of Jeb, she is the stronghorse of the play. Ironically, the victim to her papa's advances, she is the rock of these four youths. She is both the maternal figure as well as the sexy ingenue. She is every man's dream. She may be the "straight man" to Clementine's antics, but her dry remarks will stitch her a fine sweater of her own comic life. Penny must be willing to cut herself open, reveal her ugly secret, and maintain her strength to avoid a "woe is me," ending. She is beyond her years both in ambition, maturity, and pain. As the others, she can be delightfully carefree and grotesquely tortured. She is never to be played as a superficial air-brained floozy. She is as real as the dirt under her nails in her constant attempt to stay clean in this filthy place we call The Dustbowl.

PLAYWRIGHT'S NOTES

This play has a few traps in the barn. And with the utmost respect, I pull the gold from my pockets I saved from the first rehearsals and performances, and I humbly pass it on to you.

I can't say enough about making the situation and the characters "real." These are four young southern farmers. They should take their dire circumstances seriously, and stay away from southern stereotypes and slapstick interpretations. If the brothers and the sisters don't believe their characters are poignant and deep, neither will the audience. And without the depth, the awesome dark edges, you will only have a cartoon with a cliché voice.

Note that the characters of QUINCY KRANSICKLE (and his dog), GRADY GUNTHER, and EMMET EMERSON are never seen, except through the eyes of Penny and Clementine. They should be placed in the audience (in the field) and the sisters should make these offstage characters very specific, so that the audience can see them through their eyes. These characters were not written for any actor to portray, but for the audience to imagine what they look like.

The humor is black as it comes, and built on the ominous irony roaming the fields of Act One and Act Two. The laughs will come, and are the most rewarding when they are not at the expense of these extraordinary southern folks. The audience should laugh and cry because they identify with the romance, the loss, and the monster of change that eats through the lives of these characters.

The tricky tonal shifts from "comedy" to "tragedy" should be maps for the actors, with the emotional breakdown at the end of each act being a treasure. There are a few hairpin turns-- enjoy them, ride them for the pure experience of being at the mercy of your kin and your surroundings.

Act One is considered to be "The Boys' Act." Due to the loneliness, the deterioration of hope, and the inevitable death of the crop... the stillness should be deafening at times. The trick is making the non-activity an activity in itself. This is the beauty of "nothin'," as far as the eye can see. In Oklahoma, they know how to make something out of nothing better than anyone.

Act Two is, of course, "The Girls' Act." With this in mind, the focus shifts from a male point of view to a female point of view. Act One is mirrored in Act Two, just as the girls are mirrored in the boys. Go to the raw, the dark, the horrific, with a fire that will indeed be your savior. Take your time with these moments, and every Okie that ever lifted their head up out of the dust for one last breath will gasp another through you.

The poetic nature of the play should make us see these people of the land in another way, with a love for the music of their words. The lull of these farmers' rhythm should rock the audience in their cradle, as well as provide sweet honey to their ears. The dialect will come naturally when you let it sink into you, like a steak's juices on a black eye. It will heal you. This is where you will find the true voice of the field, and the heartbeat of the play.

Most importantly, give the land it's due, a life. It is an overwhelming spirit, entity, and character that must be felt like an ocean to these four suffocating fish. The field is their breath, their meal, and their curse.

I wrote the folks of Oklahoma in the way that I know them. I believe that they have a true poetic charm and beauty all their own. The simple mixed with the profound is the stalk of this play, with the broken dreams wrapping like vines around this macabre place called "The New Sahara." I hope that you plow the heart of these lost souls, as I have. To preserve the language, the emotion, the sadness, the depression, the hopelessness, and the desperate faces of these four farmers is an experience unlike any other. These folks loved their land more than life itself, and loved their kin something fierce. These two forces are the flesh and blood of this journey called "Onionheads." This was written for them...for the families and the fields that kissed each other goodnight and good-bye, forever and ever. They may now finally rest. The dust is off their boots.

Spend some time in the dirt, warsh yerself clean, then come to the table.

Thankee kindly,

Jesse Miller

ACT I SET

The Tidwell Farm is one of the many dilapidated farms that struggled for survival during the Depression and the Great Dustbowl of Oklahoma. The house was built in the early 1900's and shows a sagging posture due to weather, age, and the pain passing through it, from generations of Tidwells.

Upstage on the creaking porch, elevated by several steps, there sit two old wooden chairs, bleached and splintered by the sun, each squeaking a tune with the wind. The tattered screen door is warped and slams with an anger as the dust whistles through it. A rusty horseshoe hangs in a crooked formation over the door, while a bent spoon mobile (optional) waits to announce the approaching storm. A dull, beaten scythe and pitchfork lean against the house. It is a true ghost town with the barren landscape overwhelming the poverty stricken Tidwell shanty.

Dirt covers the ground like a brown blanket. Upstage Right, a dry tumbleweed sits motionless. Upstage Left, a dead oak tree holds a drooping clothesline as a flag of surrender. Mama's brassieres, stockings, and flowered dress hang in mourning, trying to push a little color into the sad gray picture of a dying farm. A petrified yellow Labrador sits dead next to a shriveled onion, two dry weeds, and a lone empty tin can.

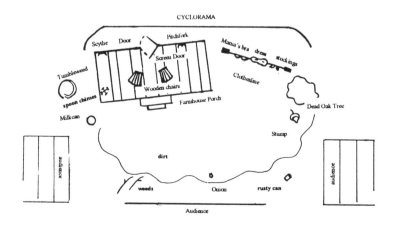

ACT II SET

The Imperial Valley Migrant Camp is one of many in which people from Oklahoma sought refuge from the dust. These camps were filled with hundreds of migrants who were forced to live in conditions that were not fit for animals. This is one of those camps.

Upstage, there are two shacks. Upstage Right is Grady Gunther's shack, a bit nicer than the upstage left Bumpinmeyer shack. After all, Grady is a supervisor, and the Bumpinmeyers are just pickers, this accounts for the difference. Nevertheless, both shacks have cardboard facings, with box sides, labeling them like fruits and vegetables. Burlap fruit sacks hang for doors. In front of Grady's shack, we see a lantern, and a stool. In front of the Bumpinmeyer shack, we see two pea picking sacks and two empty fruit crates. Between the shacks drapes a drooping clothesline holding Papa Bumpinmeyer's dirty long johns, trousers, and socks.

Downstage Right, there sits a fruit crate and a wash barrel, with a wash board inside. Dusty sits on the crate like as if it were a conquered enemy, as he plunks the banjo in the opening scene.

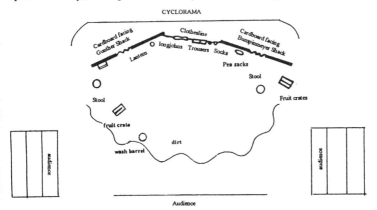

Note: To use a minimalistic set, the porch could have no farmhouse backing or door. The two shacks can be just cardboard facings. The desolation aspect of both locations and the minimalistic approach work together to suggest the loneliness, the poverty, and the depression of these lost souls.

More Winners of the American College Theatre Festival National Student Playwriting Award

Acetylene
Erik Ramsey

Blue Collar Blues
Denise Kay Dillard

The Bulldog and the Bear
Richard Gordon

The Cashier
Glen Merzer

Conpersonas
Stephen Lim

Dancers
Michael Grady

The Diviners
Revised Edition
James Leonard, Jr.

Dream at the End
of the World
Nathaniel Eaton

Eleven-Zulu
Patrick Sean Clark

Excursion Fare
Dennis Smith

Father's Prize
Poland China
Shirley Sergent

The Lower Rooms
Eliza Anderson

Prisoner
James A. Bell

The Soft Touch
Neil Cuthbert

Un Tango en la Noche
Dan Hunter

A Warring Absence
Jody Duncan

Waterworks
E. J. Safirstein

When Esther Saw
the Light
Michael Sargent

Available in SAMUEL FRENCH Acting Editions